1/22

AVID

READER

PRESS

AVID READER PRESS

New York   London   Toronto   Sydney   New Delhi

MAKING NUMBERS COUNT

The Art and Science of Communicating Numbers

CHIP HEATH
and
KARLA STARR

AVID READER PRESS
An Imprint of Simon & Schuster, Inc.
1230 Avenue of the Americas
New York, NY 10020

First Avid Reader Press hardcover edition January 2022

AVID READER PRESS and colophon are trademarks of Simon & Schuster, Inc.

For information about special discounts for bulk purchases, please contact Simon & Schuster Special Sales at 1-866-506-1949 or business@ simonandschuster.com.

Interior design by Joy O'Meara @ Creative Joy Designs

Manufactured in the United States of America

10 9 8 7 6 5 4 3 2 1

Library of Congress Cataloging-in-Publication Data has been applied for.

ISBN 978-1-9821-6544-4
ISBN 978-1-9821-6545-1 (ebook)

CONTENTS

Introduction

We both fell in love with numbers as kids, thanks to the same remarkable book, the *Guinness Book of World Records*. It was as big as a flowerpot and four times as heavy, printed in the same small type that we're reading when someone warns us to "check the fine print," but was full of extraordinary facts, stories, and most importantly *numbers*. World's largest pumpkin: 2,624 pounds. World's fastest animal: peregrine falcon, 242 miles per hour. Most forward somersaults, underwater, in one breath: 36 by Lance Davis of Los Angeles, California.

These enticing figures, of mind-boggling diversity, were the gateway to a lifelong love of numbers. The working world is full of them. From athletes to climate scientists to marketing professionals, people use numbers to measure their work, press their case, and motivate others to change.

But with all the numbers floating around, it's easy to start believing that everyone else is more on top of the numbers than we are, that somehow we missed the right class or lack the right gene, and that we are constantly at a disadvantage in understanding and using these excessively common objects.

But here's a secret: nobody really understands numbers. Nobody.

That's just a fact of being human. Our brains evolved to deal with *very small* numbers. We can recognize 1, 2, and 3 at a glance, up to 4 or 5 if we're lucky. You can get a sense of this from any kid's counting book; your brain shouts "3!" when you see a picture of 3 goldfish, no counting necessary. That's a process called *subitizing*, which our brains developed long before numerical systems were invented.[*]

Indeed, most languages in the world and throughout history have names for the numbers 1, 2, 3, 4, and 5. But after that, the supply of numbers with names runs dry, and the language is forced to resort to a generic word such as "lots" for all the other numbers—from 6 and 7 on up to a billion gazillion.[†] Picture the day-to-day frustration of trying to communicate in a culture that doesn't have words for numbers past 5:

Scene 1:

"Did we get enough eggs today to feed our people?"

"Well, we got lots of eggs. But on the other hand, we've got lots of people. So I guess we'll find out at dinnertime."

Scene 2:

"You said you'd trade me lots of pistachios for my feather necklace."

"This is lots."

"Yeah, but I meant, like, lots-lots."

And more than the frustration, imagine the out-and-out tragedies that could accrue when your culture hasn't given you words for describing critical plans using numbers.

---

[*]   There's an extensive set of endnotes that provide links to the academic research, sources for facts, and sample calculations.

[†]   This is another place where you might want to look for an endnote.

Scene 3:

"I've told you lots of times, it's lots of miles across the desert and it takes lots of days, so we'd better bring lots of water!"

"I did bring lots."

"Well, it wasn't enough lots! Now, what are our chances of reaching the oasis before we die of thirst?'

"One chance in, er, lots."

So it was a great advance when humans developed additional tools for doing math—first, systems for counting (scratches on a stone, knots on string, bar codes); then numbers (455 or 455,000); then mathematics. But while our cultural math infrastructure has changed, our brains are still the same from a biological perspective. Even if we train a lot—and we do all the way up through college—mathematics is a blisteringly new piece of high-tech software strapped on top of a clunky piece of hardware. It can work, but it will never be our first instinct. Billions, trillions, millions, kajillions . . . they all sound the same but describe wildly different realities. Our brains were designed to grok 1, 2, 3, 4, and 5. After that, it's just "lots."

Consider this thought experiment designed to help people understand the difference between "a million" and "a billion." You and a friend each enter a lottery with several large prizes. But there's a catch: If you win, you must spend $50,000 of your prize money each day until it runs out. You win a million dollars. Your friend wins a billion. How long does it take each of you to spend your lottery windfall?

As a millionaire, your encounter with runaway consumerism is surprisingly short. You go bust after a mere 20 days. If you win on Thanksgiving, you're out of money more than a week before Christmas. (Sorry, Cousin Ana, the lottery money ran out before we bought your present, but we did get you the Orange Crush umbrella!)

For your billionaire friend, resources would hold out a tad longer. He or she would have a full-time job spending $50,000 a day for . . .

55 years.

Approximately two generations. Almost 14 presidential terms. One wait to hear your name called at the DMV.

1 billion—1,000,000,000—is a number. We might think we understand it because it's right there, in black and white, but it has so many zeros that our brains fog up. It's just "lots." When we see how much larger it is than a million, it comes as a surprise.

Think of what we accomplished by forcing you to imagine watching your friend spend $50,000 every day for 55 years. Not only does it make the number click, it morphs our envy into something so real and palpable that we'll help you kick your friend in the shins. It's an animated picture that brings the number to life.

This book is based on a simple observation: we lose information when we don't translate numbers into instinctive human experience. We do hard, often painstaking work to generate the right numbers to help make a good decision—but all that work is wasted if those numbers never take root in the minds of the decision makers. As lovers of numbers, we find this tragic. The work that is being done to understand the most meaningful things in the world—ending poverty, fighting disease, conveying the scale of the universe, telling a heartbroken teen how many other times they will fall in love—is being lost because of the lack of translation.

That's when the two of us—Chip, a business school professor, and Karla, a science journalist—thought, There ought to be a book for this sort of thing.

But there isn't. We've looked. There are great guides for making graphs more stylish and persuasive, or for making infographics that make a complex process easier to understand. But there's no guidebook and writing guide for the fundamental process of making numbers count—getting people to understand them in instinctive and accurate terms.

And because we don't understand the process, we fear it. When numbers come up, half of us say, "I'm a designer/teacher/lawyer, not a numbers person," as if casting a spell to ward off a vampire. And the other half of us mumble apologies for the numbers and rush through our presentations before we slink back to our underworld lairs, where we can calculate in peace without facing scorn.

Our claim is that we aren't so different. If we simply translated our numbers differently, a lot more people would consider themselves numbers people. After all, there isn't really a choice. We encounter numbers *lots* of times in a given day. Our economy, our schedules, our transportation system, our household management, everything we do is based around numbers. We can choose to be involved with numerical decisions or stay in the dark, but we can't actually opt out. What we can do is ask that they make sense to us—we're only human.

It could even be fun. After all, the *Guinness Book of World Records* was not created to be an academic textbook. It was created to settle bar bets (yes, it is *that* Guinness, the company that makes beer so thick you can prop up a spoon in it).

But business first. Let's look at a case study of a number being translated in more and less effective ways. We'll start with a raw statistic that we found pretty shocking:

> The U.S. government has a 5 A Day campaign that's designed to encourage kids to eat five servings of fruits and vegetables a day. McDonald's alone outspends this campaign by a ratio of 350 to 1.

Anyone reading that sees a huge disparity in favor of the fast-food message. But initially, that's all we see—just one form of "lots." We know the fast-food companies have big ad budgets, we know that they outspend healthy messages, but 20 times more, 143 times more, 350 times more? What's the big deal?

The higher numbers get, the less sensitive we get to them, a phenomenon psychologists have labeled "psychophysical numbing." Moving on the number scale from 10 to 20 feels significant. But moving an equal distance from 340 to 350, even though it's the same increase, we feel nothing . . . that's "numbing."

Our goal in this book is to give you some techniques that are going to improve your odds of overcoming that numbing. We believe you can use the principles of psychology to help people understand and act on a number. And that requires translation.

There are many possible ways to translate a sentence or paragraph from one language to another. Some will better convey the meaning, some may be more precise, some may even be more beautiful. Well, the same is true of number translations. Consider two alternative ways of translating the fact above:

Comparison Set 1:

Translation A.	Translation B.
McDonald's alone outspends the 5 A Day campaign by 350 to 1.	For every 5 hours and 50 minutes a child spends watching McDonald's commercials, they spend 1 minute on 5 A Day.

Translation B is better. We care about kids more than "outspending." The money budget is now converted to time. Breaking 350 down into hours and minutes makes it feel a little bigger, a little more concrete, a little more crazy.

But Translation B could be improved. 5 hours, 50 minutes is a big block of time, and it's not how children watch commercials. They don't see them one after the other—they see them sprinkled into their shows, again and again and again. Translation D below is designed to account for that insight.

Comparison Set 2:

Translation C.	Translation D.
McDonald's alone outspends the 5 A Day campaign by 350 to 1.	If a child sees a McDonald's commercial every single day, it would take them almost a year to see just one commercial about 5 A Day.

Calendar time is easier to feel than number counts. We know what a day is, and we know what a year is. Even young children know there is a *lonnnnnnng* time between birthday parties. Whenever we can translate a number into calendar time, we're able to work with numbers we fundamentally understand. Nobody ever said, "I'm not really a calendar person."

(By the way, the colored boxes above follow a format you'll see a lot in the text. A box generally provides two translations. One presents a number the standard way, as people might normally present it. The other is translated using one of our techniques to help you make your numbers more understandable and usable. Our recommended technique is always in the shaded box which will typically be on the right.)

Pro tip: *If you just want to get your creative juices flowing, thumb through the book and look at our examples. You may get some* *ideas from seeing the techniques in action. Go ahead, take a moment and look through some of the examples in the colored boxes before you proceed.*

The McDonald's translations illustrate something that we'll see over and over in this book. Although our brains may not be prepared for numbers such as "112 times more" (or "a million"), there is probably a part of our well-trained cultural mind that has very good intuition about the number we're having a hard time understanding. So we may do better if we translate 112 to clock time (1 hour, 52 minutes) or calendar time (every day for almost four months). We've come to believe, after working with these principles for years, that almost every gnarly number has something—an analogy, a comparison, another dimension—that will allow us to translate it into something we can remember, use, and discuss with others.

We pulled the McDonald's example from our "Avoid numbing by converting your number to a process that unfolds over time" chapter, which is just one of more than 30 translation techniques we focus on throughout the book. Each chapter introduces a simple concept, illustrates it with a few examples from business or science or sports, and explores one or two nuances. We designed the book to work as a training manual (when you're first trying your hand at translation), and also as an "I need inspiration now!" reference to thumb through when you're trying to translate an important number and you get stuck.

Where did these techniques come from? For the last 15 years, Chip has taught an MBA class on making ideas stick—mostly to MBAs, but also to physicians, artists, Naval commanders, and scientists. For years, he suggested avoiding numbers whenever possible. One semester, there was a student who challenged this advice. "I'm an investment banker. All of my ideas involve numbers. I can't escape them." So that year, Chip added a class devoted to making numbers stick.

The first session put the "error" in "trial and error." Arming his students with a set of dry statistics, Chip gave them one hour to come up with their best translations. The results were . . . uninspiring. Worse than uninspiring. They were awful. Rather than making numbers easier to grasp, the analytical MBAs often came up with a complex analogy from a loosely related domain that made the numbers harder to understand or made them seem less important.

Chip kept tinkering, hoping that with the right setup the students would arrive at some basic principles of numerical communication. After all, they were MBAs and engineers who worked every day with numbers. He didn't want to constrain their creativity by sharing too prematurely the few ideas he had at that time for making numbers count.

Finally, he gave up trying to facilitate discovery and instead described a few basic principles right before the exercises. Immediately, the results changed. The students not only grasped the concepts but ran with them, coming up with some brilliant applications.

The basic principles for communicating numbers are simple, but not obvious, even if they might feel that way once you grasp them. They're hard to discover, but not hard to remember. The trick is knowing that there *are* basic principles, ones that can be used again and again.

The class became one of the most enjoyable days of the quarter. Someone would come up with a clever translation and the class would go, "*Ooooooooohhhhhh.*" Once, a group of students we'll describe later actually got applause . . . for a number translation!

In doing this book we had the advantage of casting a broad net. We searched the social sciences in psychology, anthropology, and sociology. We read books and papers about the development of math ability (and where our deficits are). We looked at what anthropologists discovered about how various cultures handle numbers. We searched history, science, and journalism for techniques that make numbers count.

Over the years, our principles have been road-tested by some of the planet's most skeptical and analytical minds—MBAs, engineering students, and New Yorkers. And they can be used by anyone who has mastered basic math; we've seen them work for middle schoolers.

The book is intended to be helpful to people at all levels of numerical fluency, or numeracy. You can rest assured that learning the principles won't require any computations that can't be done with a simple calculator—the old-fashioned kind with just a few giant buttons.

This, unfortunately, may be the first time anyone has bothered to show you that numbers can (and should) be translated. Think about it: in school, you were force-fed cardinal numbers and polynomial factoring and a thousand other topics, but there was never a lesson on How to Communicate Numbers. (Pop quiz: Which skill turned out to be more important in the work world?)

If you're one of the rare numerically savvy people, someone who loved the *Guinness Book of World Records* as a kid and who took the extra math classes (and kind of liked them), these principles will also be invaluable for you. Often experts become so accustomed to their own wizardry that they no longer see how much work it takes for the rest of us to do what they do. Researchers call this "the Curse of Knowledge," and it is the supervillain in any communication domain. When experts are asked to communicate something they understand intimately—musicians tapping out the rhythm of familiar songs, statisticians presenting shocking graphs, your dog barking to alert you to a *really* interesting smell—they wildly overestimate how much of their mental model of the world is shared by their audience.

The practices in this book, because they work with our natural instincts, can help experts cursed with their knowledge translate their expertise into a blessing. Math can reveal truths about the world that the human mind was never built to intuitively grasp. If you can use math, you have a valuable skill. If you can use it and make it clear, bringing what is obscure and distant into the range where others can see it and feel it—well, then you have a super-power. Superman could see through walls; you can make the walls invisible so everyone else can see through them.

And for the non-experts, just understanding the simple trick of translation is like a judo or jiujitsu skill that gives you a fighting chance against even the most skilled numbers people. Know how to ask for the right translation—"Can you put that in concrete terms?" "What is that per employee per day?" "If this flip chart represents our total budget, can you draw me a rectangle that represents the size of this expense?"—and you put yourself back in the game. Opponents won't be able to snow you with a blizzard of numbers anymore. And analytical people of good faith will appreciate having a worthy sparring partner, pleasantly surprised that the seemingly artsy HR person has a mathematical edge.

It's hard to imagine someone who wouldn't benefit from this power: Picture a manager arguing for a bigger budget for testing a product with consumers. A scientist trying to convey the distance between two points in the universe. A marketer demonstrating a campaign's potential outreach. A coach discussing the benefits of practicing a few more minutes each day. Our world increasingly features numbers that lie beyond the scope of our intuition. They pop up in every area of business (from R&D to customer service), and are at the center of almost all human endeavor (consider science, sports, and government).

We live in a world in which our success often depends on our ability to make numbers count.

TRANSLATE EVERYTHING, FAVOR USER-FRIENDLY NUMBERS

Translate Everything

Here's a quick test of whether you are handling numbers correctly: Go through your letter, document, or PowerPoint deck. Circle each number and then look above and below by one paragraph or bullet point and find the phrase where you translate the number. For example:

>> "To put that in context . . ."
>> "To put that in perspective . . ."
>> "What that means is . . ."
>> "Think of it this way . . ."
>> "That means . . ."
>> "By comparison . . ."

If you see phrases like these, then the number is likely helping you make your point. If you don't, you've left it in a foreign language and neglected to translate. As one would say in Japanese, *"Darekani kaiwani hairenaito kanjisaseru kotoha shitsurei desu."*

Numbers aren't the natural language for humans—in the United States, in Japan, or anywhere. If you're filling in databases, it's fine to leave numbers as numbers, but the second you want to use numbers in an argument or presentation, it's your job to put them in human terms.*

Two scientists at Microsoft Research, Jake Hofman and Dan Goldstein, believe in this idea so strongly that they've spent the better part of a decade spearheading a project known as the Perspectives Engine with a simple goal: develop tools that make numbers easier for humans to understand.

Microsoft's search engine, Bing, delivers millions of facts a day in response to queries. The Perspectives team wondered whether some simple contextual phrases would help people understand and remember their numerical search results.

So they did something basic: Instead of just reporting that Pakistan has an area of 340,000 square miles, they added a brief "perspective phrase," something like "that's about the size of 2 Californias." And then, at time scales ranging from a few minutes later to a few weeks later, they tested people to see if they remembered the fact they had been shown.

Some perspective phrases were better than others. Simpler comparisons from more familiar states or countries led to better memory for the facts. But ALL phrases were better than nothing. Even a slightly unwieldy comparison was more effective than a number alone.

In fact, adding a single perspective phrase cut the error rates in half when people tried to recall the facts. That doesn't mean every guess was a bull's-eye. There were still plenty of errors. But people were at least hitting the dartboard, not the poster next to it on the wall.

By putting a little thought into translation, accuracy essentially doubled. That's an eye-popping effect. To put this in perspective,

---

* If you're waiting for a translation of the Japanese phrase, it's coming—but keep in mind how you feel right now, while you're waiting.

imagine what a CFO would pay to have their key metric recalled twice as much by investors on earnings calls, or how much a history teacher would be willing to work to double his students' recall of critical historical facts. And yet here, you can do it with a snap of your fingers. Translation is even more than a quality-control supertool—it also helps build strong relationships. When people don't "get" a number, they not only miss the number itself but also feel more distanced from you and your presentation. They may tune out and miss the message. Worse, they may even tune *you* out, because you've failed to build rapport that makes them feel included. (See there—you never expected to get relationship advice from a book about numbers! Perhaps taking Calculus 3 might have helped you spend fewer years on dating apps!)

As one would say in Japanese, *"Darekani kaiwani hairenaito kanjisaseru kotoha shitsurei desu."* "It's rude to make people feel they're being excluded from a conversation."* You may have felt it just a little when we didn't translate this phrase earlier. You may have felt it at a snotty restaurant, a pretentious dinner party, or anytime your friends went on with some inside joke about an event you didn't attend.

Numbers are only fun if they make sense to everyone. Be a good neighbor. Translate!

---

* This phrase is not a long-standing cultural proverb, just an important observation.

Avoid Numbers: Perfect Translations Don't Need Numbers

"Avoid numbers." That recommendation might surprise you, as if we were starting our cookbook with a warning: STEP AWAY FROM THE FOOD. But the overall goal with a number translation is to relay a *message*, and that goal doesn't always require numbers.

If you've ever returned from an extended trip overseas, you know the oddly comforting feeling of seeing airport signs in your native tongue: *Baggage claim. Food court. Exit.*

Math is no one's native tongue. At best, it's a second language, picked up in school through formal teaching. The more you can relay your message in the native song of your people—*without* math—the better.

The secret to translating numbers is simple: avoid using them. Translate them into concrete, vivid, meaningful messages that are clear enough to make numbers unnecessary.

The next example is from Karla's middle-school days, in a science class about ecology. The example tries to get across how very little water is drinkable despite the fact that the world is filled with water. Here's the numbers-intensive version of the statistics.

97.5% of the world's water is salinated. Of the 2.5% that's fresh, over 99% is trapped in glaciers and snowfields. In total, only .025% of the water on the globe is actually drinkable by humans and animals.

The original statistic is compelling—but it's unmemorable. However, over two decades later, Karla remembered a translation of those facts into a thought experiment that was simple and concrete. Here it is:

Imagine a gallon jug filled with water with three ice cubes next to it. All of the water in the jug is salt water. The ice cubes are the only fresh water, and humans can only drink the drops that are melting off of each.

This message made it into the book because Karla remembered it two decades later—the shock of "getting" (really, thoroughly understanding) a deep truth about the world; the fun of relaying the analogy to parents, older siblings, and adult friends and watching them react with surprise.

Let's pause for a second and give respect to the teacher or scientist or journalist who originally created that translation. That's a message so simple that it needs no numbers and so profound that it still gets invoked among adults who studied it as a middle schooler.

If you're not a numbers person, the gallon-jug translation is instantly more approachable. In the first translation, when you see all the percent signs and the small decimal, you may go into panic mode. You might even have put the book down and not be reading this right now.

In the gallon-jug translation, you feel confident, not only that you could understand the example but that you could explain it to someone else. No thinking *Is it .0025% or .25%? Which one was 97.5% and which one was 99%?* Gallon jug, ice cubes, drop of water each. Easy.

If you *are* a numbers person, you might initially mourn the loss of some beautiful statistics. But the statistics are still there—they're just below the surface, under the hood. Now others can appreciate their beauty. And, as someone who understands both the numbers and the way our minds work, you can create a picture of a key environmental fact that can stay in people's minds for decades.

Let's look at another example . . .

The largest volcano in the solar system, Olympus Mons on Mars, is about 300,000 square kilometers in area and about 22 kilometers (14 miles) tall.	The largest volcano in the solar system, Olympus Mons on Mars, covers an area as big as Arizona or Italy. It's so tall that if you tried to fly over it during a normal cross-country plane flight, you'd crash into it halfway up the slope.

You might be tempted to make an apples-to-apples comparison here, and say Olympus Mons is more than twice the height of Mount Everest. But what is Everest to most of us? It's something we read about. It's rare we meet even one person who's seen it directly (if we did, we'd know—they'd never shut up about it).

A cross-country flight, on the other hand, is familiar—the smell of filtered air, the tiny, never acknowledged, battles for extra centimeters on the shared elbow rest, the landscape gliding by below us, so tiny and distant. We can imagine how weird it would be to run into something that didn't just rise to meet us but towered to twice our height. And if we flew past it for as long as it took to cross Arizona (if we fly domestic) or Italy (if we're international), it would be a truly otherworldly experience. Imagining it helps us grasp the alienness of Mars.

Moving back to Earth, in 2018, the *New York Times* published a long article showing data, field by field (politics, Hollywood, journalism), that demonstrated how far our society is from equality. But rather than quoting a dense wall of numbers, they cleverly illustrated the disparities by using some striking comparisons.

A very small percentage of Fortune 500 CEOs are women.	Among Fortune 500 CEOs, there are more men named James than there are women.

A week from now, you'd be hard-pressed to remember a specific number for the percentage of female CEOs. But you could get a ballpark estimate—something more like 5% than 20%—from the basic fact. You might not even remember the name (John? David? Steve?), but you'd remember that it outnumbered a whole gender. That feels so deeply wrong. You shouldn't be able to ask "On the CEO panel this afternoon, is there a James?" and have better odds of getting a yes reply than if you ask "Is there a woman?"

This is a case where the numbers themselves would be distracting. Doing the right research to come up with the James comparison is essential, but once you have such a surprising result, elaborating that the population as a whole has 50.8% women or 1.682% Jameses just distracts from the point.

Consider one final example, about racial inequality: 2 Black and 2 White male test subjects visited businesses to fill out job applications for positions that were listed in a local newspaper. Half of the time, subjects wrote that they had a felony drug conviction and served 18 months in prison.

34% of White applicants and 14% of Black applicants without records received callbacks, compared to 17% and 5% with records.	White job applicants who had served jail time for a felony were more likely to receive a callback than were Black applicants with impeccable records.

The first translation seems to tell you something you likely already know: that racism is real and significant. For both sets of applicants, with or without a felony record, White applicants fared better than Black applicants by a large margin.

But how long would you have to stare at those numbers to figure out the translation on the right—that there wasn't just discrimination across categories, but that Black applicants with no record were treated *worse* than White applicants who had served time for a felony?

The comparison makes viscerally clear the scale of the barrier racism puts up. A White reader can imagine what it would be like to be treated as a felon—it's a gut punch to realize that in the job market, an applicant would be treated worse than that solely for being Black.

Without the translation, we may lose the audience before the gut punch can land. A reader is likely to skim the stats, get a surface-level reading, and move on, without ever grasping the strongest point.

If you think you have a statistic that says something important, skip the middleware: say the important thing directly. You want people to see and *feel* the numbers, not just read them.

Try Focusing On 1 at a Time

The quickest route to having people understand your number is to start with something simple, a well-understood part of the overall scene: 1 employee, citizen, or student. 1 business, marriage, or classroom. 1 deal, game, or day. Focus on 1 concrete chunk of an experience: 1 prototypical visit, 1 day, 1 month in the quarter.

If that very simple setup makes your point, declare victory! You can end there.

Throughout the first 18 years of his career in the NBA, LeBron James scored over 35,000 points.	Throughout the first 18 years of his career in the NBA, LeBron James scored an average of over 27 points per game.

Our temptation is to go for the staggering number. "Wow, that is *big*." 35,000 feels huge. 27 doesn't. At least not at first.

This misconception is something we have labeled "big-ism." We are tempted to go for something bigger when what we really need is something with a size we can understand. "Big as a bus" makes intuitive sense—we've seen one and know it can squash us. "Big as a galaxy" has less heft. Although it's technically larger, that doesn't mean much because we've never dealt directly with a galaxy. (Apologies, Milky Way, present company excluded.)

In the case of LeBron James, we don't know how many points players typically accumulate during a basketball career. But we do know 27 points in one game. It means you were on fire that night. If that's your average night, for high school or college, well, that means you're really good at basketball. If you maintain that through 18 years of NBA play, well, that means you're *frickin' good* at basketball. But we can only see that by looking at the typical game. That is the power of 1.

There are about 400 million civilian-owned firearms in the United States.	There are about 330 million citizens in the United States, and more than 400 million firearms . . . or enough for every man, woman, and child to own 1, and still have around 70 million firearms left over.

It's unsurprising that a large country with many gun enthusiasts would have lots of guns—which is all that "400 million" says at first. "There are *lots* of guns in America." But once we turn those guns into *people with guns*, we start to engage with how far beyond reason our armament level is. It makes us imagine every child and toddler having their own. Shotguns on the side of cribs, Glocks color-coordinated to match your niece's princess outfit. And after all that, enough guns left over to furnish a sizable army. In fact, you could equip each active-duty serviceperson, every soldier, sailor, and pilot, with 52 firearms.

The abstract "400 million" number started to click when we started matching it down to the basic unit. One person with a gun. One game of basketball. Test-drive LeBron's scoring prowess per game or our national firearm figures per person, and your reaction is: "That's crazy!" Crazy in a good way for the basketball legend, but in a terrifying way for the gun-toting infant.

So far we've focused on 1 as taking the average. But "1" can also mean a typical case study—not an average so much as a single, representative example. Our brains process stories better than statistics.

In Bangladesh, millions survive on pennies a day. With little access to banks, they're forced to pay outrageous interest rates (100% a year or more) whenever they need to access money.

Muhammad Yunus—an economics professor in Bangladesh—scoured the streets of a village to locate every resident who worked with moneylenders. In total, those 42 villagers were borrowing $27. Using just his paycheck as a professor, he loaned the 42 villagers the sums they would normally borrow from the moneylenders.

One woman, who wove beautiful bamboo stools, borrowed 22 cents from Yunus for her day's materials. Freed of the outrageous interest her moneylender charged her for her 1-day loan, she was able to take home more than the 2 cents a day she had made in the past and still have enough to pay Yunus back in short order. From there, she used the surplus to improve her family's nutrition and housing, and her children's schooling. This story happened over and over for the villagers to whom Yunus loaned money. The repayment rate was 100%.

"Poverty in Bangladesh" feels hopelessly large and complex. The overall problem is depressing, but the power of 1 is that it focuses us on the tinier day-to-day components of the overall problem in a way that shows us the potential for progress. Widespread poverty feels hopeless. But in two simple stories, this translation showed the potential for action.

First, we look at one village, where one person, Yunus, was able to make a donation. Then we look at the impact of this on one artisan, to trace in detail how the process transformed her life.

From one villager, we can understand the impact of one lender who affected 41 other people. From this one lender, we can understand the impact of widespread microfinance. If we could organize such donations in a systematic way, we could change the reality for many families, a reality that would never be visible in the aggregate.

The U.S. national debt is $27 trillion.*	The U.S. national debt is $27 trillion—$82,000 per citizen.

Our brains spin when we try to envision a trillion dollars. But focusing on 1 helps us understand the scale of the issue—and it gives us something to work with. $82,000 is a lot of money, but over the long run, could it pay off if we invest it wisely?

In our personal lives, we Americans take on debts of that magnitude in order to buy a house, start a business, or fund an education. Are there things we could invest in as a nation that might make undertaking this kind of debt worthwhile? Scientific discovery, good

* The current value. No matter what we use here, it will be out of date by the time you read it.

relations with neighbors, preserving our land? $27 trillion stops the conversation; $82k might start it, spurring a conversation about quality and strategy of spending instead of a panic.

Try a prototype: We often collect so much data that the accretion of random details blurs our picture. When confronted with a whole table full of data, challenge yourself to capture as much as you can in one scenario. We might call the result of this exercise "a prototype," which is the most central or typical member of a category. For birds, a robin is a prototype of what we expect to see when we see a bird. Less so a hawk (chest too broad, talons too lethal), a flamingo (too tall, too bright, unusual feeding position), or an ostrich (need we explain?).

Consider what a brand of fast-preparation food might learn from turning all its demographic and psychographic information into a unified picture of its prototypical consumer:

Our median customer is 32 years old, married, with kids; and 93% of our customers work a full-time job. Our typical customer has 1.7 children (with 1.3 under the age of five). Her top 3 reasons for buying our product are 1) convenience, 2) familiar flavor, and 3) "not as bad" nutritionally as many of our competitors.

Our prototypical customer is a 32-year-old mom stopping by the store on the way home from work after picking her kids up from day care. She is going down the aisles with a 2-year-old in the cart and a 4-year-old walking beside her. She has to grab the box she wants for dinner without the 4-year-old unloading the shelf closest to him. And when she tries to read the ingredients in fine print, the 2-year-old is slapping the box out of her hand.

After considering our prototypical customer, we recommend simplifying the package design, so people can locate their favorite flavor faster, and increasing the font size of our nutritional information.

The string of statistics in the first example doesn't cohere and doesn't produce much insight.

But when the numbers take the shape of one human, we can start to feel and understand their implications. We don't empathize with a marketing demographic; we empathize with a person. We have vast experience with stepping into a story, from our first picture books to the last Hollywood movie we watched. But we've never been trained to step into a distribution. A prototype can embody a ream of data, yet remind us that the data merely represents our real customer—one whose children pitch tantrums in grocery stores just like ours do.

You have to do the right analysis to get the right answer. But when you convey the right answer, you don't have to use the numbers you used to get the right answer. In fact, the most perfect translations of the numbers may have no numbers at all.

Favor User-Friendly Numbers

Perform the following experiment on yourself, then on a friend who will humor you for 90 seconds. Glance at List A for a few seconds, close your eyes, and say the numbers out loud. Repeat for List B.

List A	List B
2,842,900	3 million
5.73 times bigger	6 times bigger
9/17	1/2

Which list did you remember better? If you said "List A," you probably forgot which was A. The second list is easier to deal with in every way: it's easier to understand, easier to retain, and easier to repeat.

And the information it conveys is functionally the same. That new office that's 6 times bigger won't feel any less spacious if you find it's only 5.73 times bigger. And try telling someone who got only half as much pay for the same amount of work someone else did that they actually got 9/17ths as much. See if they feel better.

Looking one more time at Lists A and B, now let's *do something* with the numbers you just tried to remember. Suppose we told you that the first row is current profit for your partnership, and—fantasy-time here—the last row is your cut. How much money do you stand to make this year?

List B delivers the happy news of $1.5 million in your pocket (and delivers it quickly).

List A delivers . . . quite slowly . . . wait for it . . . news of $1,505,065. (You know, about $1.5 million.) By the time you've done the calculation, the conversation has likely moved on.

There are two reasons to favor user-friendly numbers. The first is that they're friendly! People like to feel included in the conversation, and they don't like needless work. It's just impolite to make them jump through hoops on the way to grasping your point.

The second is that they're effective. If you don't consider yourself a people person, think of it as an engineering challenge. The numbers in List B are designed to fit the hardware of our brain, which has a hard limit to what it can process. Psychologist George A. Miller wrote one of the most famous papers in psychology after asking himself, How big is human working memory?

His answer was in the title of his paper: "The Magical Number 7, Plus or Minus 2." That number was the limit for how many things we could hold in our short-term memory. Whether it's numbers, names, digits, or anything else, if we have to memorize more than 7 pieces of info (sometimes just 5, or up to 9), we start to lose track.

In fact, a single unfriendly number can crash the system all on its own. Think of a complicated fraction (17/139), multidigit number (4,954,287), or long decimal (.092383). These numbers only measure one thing, but take up many slots in our memory. Even if we manage to memorize them, we have no room to remember anything else, and the message is lost.

More often than not, we don't even make sense of the complicated number in the first place. Alfred Taubman, former CEO of the A&W restaurant chain and author of *Threshold Resistance*, learned that lesson the hard way when his company tried to introduce a third-pound burger at the same price as the McDonald's quarter-pounder. More than half the customers thought they were being ripped off. "Why should we pay the same amount for less meat?" they said.

The value of the new A&W burger depended on consumers comparing two fractions: 1/3 and 1/4. But fractions are difficult for everyone, because they're parts of things as opposed to whole objects. We like to count things, and fractions don't equal "things." So, we jump to the closest available whole numbers. 4 is bigger than 3, so we mistakenly infer that a 1/4-pounder is a bigger burger than a 1/3-pounder.

There are lots of nuances to making numbers user-friendly and avoiding mistakes like these. The appendix has a more complete set of examples. But you can avoid most mistakes with these two rules of thumb, and a caveat:

Rule #1. Simpler Is Better: Round with Enthusiasm.

4.736 is about 5.
    5/11 is about half.
    217 is about 200.
We learn rounding when we're first trying to get the hang of math. Then we tend to forget it, as we get addicted to calculators and spreadsheets.

But people in the professions that master numbers—physicists, engineers, doctors—always return to rounding. A lot of the work they do is really just translating complicated numbers back into simple ones, so they can get the hang of a problem and talk it through with other people. They have terms for this kind of conscious simplification: "back-of-the-envelope calculation," a "quick-and-dirty" analysis, a "ballpark" number. Precision has a time and a place, but with the typical project, the times when precision carries the day are probably far fewer than the times that demand a judicious *im*precision.

Remember the Perspectives Engine team at Microsoft who found that just a single perspective phrase doubled the accuracy with which people could recall and use facts about geography? They also conducted experiments that confirmed the value of rounding, by testing readers on competing versions of facts from the *New York Times*: one version with unrounded numbers, and one with heavily rounded numbers.

The example below deals with the Frick Collection, a museum that was proposing a controversial expansion. Here are excerpts from the two versions the Perspectives Engine tested.

Precise version: Of the 40,100 square feet the Frick wants to add, only 3,990 of it would be for showing art—the size of an oligarch's wine cellar, in that neighborhood.

Rounded number version: Of the 40,000 square feet the Frick wants to add, only 4,000 of it would be for showing art—the size of an oligarch's wine cellar, in that neighborhood.

After seeing several passages from the *Times*, participants were challenged to recall the numbers they had initially seen and to perform some computation with them. Only 2 out of 5 readers who'd seen the precise version were able to remember the figures accurately,[*] compared with 3 out of 5 readers who'd seen the

---

[*] Defined in this case as within 10% of the figure.

rounded version. When they were asked to perform a calculation—in this case, what percentage of the addition would go to showing art—the readers who'd seen the rounded numbers again beat their counterparts who'd seen the precise but less user-friendly numbers.

Across six different subject areas, and with almost 1,000 participants, the experiments got consistent results: rounded numbers meant more successful recall and fewer computation mistakes, while precise numbers meant more forgetfulness and more errors.

The findings were consistent with Miller's observations. There's a limit to what we can remember. Feeding precise numbers into a machine that isn't designed to work with them is counterproductive. If you value accuracy, use rounded, user-friendly numbers. Rounding early means sharper recall in the end.

Rule #2. Concrete Is Better: Use Whole Numbers to Describe Whole Objects, Not Decimals, Fractions, or Percentages.

Whole numbers—numbers you can count—feel real. We can imagine them as whole objects, things our hunter-gatherer brains can work with.

On the other hand, partial numbers—decimals, fractions, percentages, and ratios—simply don't register as real to our minds. We may be able to work with them for a given time when we're in math mode, but if we're asked questions on the fly, we tend to have trouble grasping the concept.

In other words, anytime we give our audience figures that aren't whole numbers, the message is unlikely to make sense to them. Not only are they prone to make errors remembering and calculating the numbers, but there's a good chance they never even envision what we're describing in the first place—because the number attached isn't solid.

Use whole numbers whenever you can to make your message real. For extra fractions and decimals, this often means rounding.

For numbers less than 1, you can use a method we call "counting in baskets" to make things start to show up as whole numbers. If you find that .2% of people have a certain trait, use a basket size of at least 500, maybe 1,000, to make them show up as real people. "1 out of 500" or "2 out of 1,000" makes these abstract percentages into real things.

Make the baskets as small as you can while retaining the wholeness of whole numbers. If 2/3rds or .67 or 67% of people didn't like the new flavor, then make them feel like people in a room. "2 out of 3 people thought cheesy marshmallow was "disgusting." Going up to 67 out of 100 would dilute understanding.

But if you need to bring in multiple stats, you don't want to mix basket sizes. You want a basket small enough that it feels real and doesn't make your audience do math, but large enough that multiple stats are directly comparable. 1 *in* 6 people thought cheesy marshmallow flavor was intriguing, while 4 *in* 6 thought it was disgusting (note that we changed the basket size above so that the "2 in 3" and the "1 in 6" would live in similar-size baskets, and be easier to compare).

Rule #3. Follow the Rules But Defer to Expertise. Rules 1 and 2 May be Trumped by Expert Knowledge.

The purpose of the first two rules is to make sure your audience understands the numbers you give them. The advice is based on research about what people tend to understand or not.

But when your audience has specialized experience, they might develop shortcuts that change these general rules. Bring numbers into an audience's wheelhouse and they might be capable of more precise calculations. For example, shoppers may flail when asked to calculate .20 × 2.77 on their kids' homework assignment, but tell them there's 20% off canned tuna ($2.77) and they perform like certified accountants.

That's because people who get very familiar with certain types of numbers don't have to use as much memory to work with them.

George A. Miller's "Magical Number 7" has an expansion module, under certain conditions. We can load around 7 coherent "units" into our mental working space, but depending on our learning and expertise, those units may vary in size. Psychologists have a term for a "collection of information that gets recalled together as a unit": in an admirable feat of precise technical language, they call it a "chunk." A chunk might be one random digit, a phone prefix for downtown Houston (713), or the first two verses of your favorite song.

Experts have chunks of information that they can activate easily, and this means that Rules 1 and 2 are not universally useful. If we know our audience and how they chunk things, we can give them numbers in formats that they can easily process. What we think is confusing may be effortlessly simple to people with the right exposure. Pollsters are used to percentages, baseball fans can quote batting averages (a decimal recalled to 3 digits of precision!), and gamblers can express odds in ways that are mind-boggling to the non-gambler. Bakers, mechanics, and tailors all have their own sets of fractions that make sense to them.

Serve your audience what they know, not what would be best for someone else. Normally we would never advise that someone use a 3-digit decimal to express one of the key metrics for their business, but baseball fans have developed strong reactions to the difference between a .277 batting average and a .312 average.

Familiarity wins.

• • •

Of course, you should always break any of these rules when doing so makes things clearer. You want to trust your judgment. But as we explore the more nuanced levels of numerical communication, keep the basics in mind. Always put your best—simplest, roundest, most familiar—numbers forward when you can.

Here are a couple of exercises to work through these principles. If we counted each atom in a human body, which elements would be the most common? Consider some alternative ways of expressing this:

Hydrogen 31/50	Hydrogen 62%	For every 10 atoms in your body, 6 are hydrogen, 3 oxygen, 1 carbon. All the other elements are much less common.
Oxygen 6/25	Oxygen 24%	
Carbon 3/25	Carbon 13%	
Nitrogen 1/173	Nitrogen 1.1%	
Other 1/500	Other 0.2%	

The first column, with its unequal numbers, resembles advanced gambling odds. If you understand it, you may have a problem. (Gamblers Anonymous can help!)

The second, which uses interpretable, comparable percentages, is a little better.

But we prefer the last one, which better illustrates the concept of trace elements (it's rare when you find 'em!) and the ubiquity of the big 3 (remember that you're mostly water, 2 hydrogens, and 1 oxygen per molecule).

We close with a message from public health (one of our favorite examples, contributed by Marial Williams at a workshop for graduate students on making messages stick) that illustrates how unreal percentages can seem to our brains, and how utterly real it feels when a translation makes use of simple counting numbers.

40% of U.S. adults do not always wash their hands after using the bathroom at home.	2 out of every 5 people you shake hands with may not have washed their hands between using the toilet and touching your hands.

The 40% number doesn't feel big or visceral. So what? A minority of adults don't always wash their hands at home. Most still do.

But that "2 out of 5" combined with the clear personal scenario tells you right away why you should care. If you shook hands with 5 people, contact with the unwashed might have already happened twice. You're probably reaching for the hand sanitizer already.

Be kind to your audience. Make sure you use clean, user-friendly numbers. And clean, user-friendly hands.

TO HELP PEOPLE GRASP
YOUR NUMBERS,
GROUND THEM IN THE
FAMILIAR, CONCRETE,
AND HUMAN SCALE

Find Your Fathom: Help People Understand Through Simple, Familiar Comparisons

If you want to help people understand quickly, define your new concept in terms of something your audience already knows.

Cultures have used this formula for millennia to develop measurements. One survey of 84 cultures, from ancient Romans to the Māori, found that most cultures understood units of measurement through the human body, an omnipresent measuring stick. The length of outstretched arms, fingertip to fingertip, developed as a measurement in half of the cultures. (In English, we call this a "fathom.") One in every four cultures developed a measurement defined as the length of the forearm, called a "cubit" in Middle English; it appears in the Biblical story of Noah and his ark (which measured 300 × 50 × 30 cubits). "Mile" comes from the Latin phrase for "thousand steps."

Observe how local health campaigns around the world translated "6 feet" to relay social distancing guidelines during the COVID pandemic. Effective translations combine easily imagined comparisons with as little math as possible:

1 hockey stick—*Canada*
1 tatami mat—*Japan*
1 adult gator—*Florida*
1 surfboard—*San Diego*
1 adult cassowary—*North Queensland, Australia*
1 Michael Jordan— *imagine Michael Jordan giving you and your friend an air-five—basketball court*
1 caribou—*Yukon, Canada*
1 bear—*Russia*
1 fathom—*U.S. Navy*
1 alpaca—*Ohio county fair*
1.5 wood chippers—*North Dakota*
2 baguettes—*France*
4 trout or 1 fishing rod—*Montana*
1 surfboard, or 1-1/2 mountain bikes—*Orange County, California*
4 koalas—*Sydney, Australia*
24 buffalo wings—*Buffalo, NY*
72 pistachios—*New Mexico*

Some of these are useful; others are just cute. You've seen a hockey stick or fishing rod before. But if you've ever witnessed 24 buffalo wings or 72 pistachios end-to-end, someone needs more training in table manners.

How do you find the right measuring stick for your number? How do you find your fathom? As we have seen, Jake Hofman and Dan Goldstein studied adding number translations to facts about population and geography. With their colleague Christopher Riederer, they found that the best number translations combined a comparison that was easy to imagine and a simple scaling factor:

The geographic area of Pakistan is about the size of 5 Oklahomas.	The geographic area of Pakistan is about twice the size of California.

So to come up with your fathom, brainstorm items of a similar size that your audience would know well. If you get stuck, use the MacGyver principle. In the 1980s television show, MacGyver would use his knowledge of science to create tools that Batman or James Bond would have spent millions on. Except MacGyver built his tools out of recycled fast-food containers from lunch. The MacGyver principle is this: Look around you. See what you can build using found objects in the environment. Consider what's universally known to your people: local references, objects used in your field, items in the news.

As you search, favor objects that only need a simple multiplier. 4 koalas or 72 pistachios are tougher to work with than simple multipliers such as 2 or half. In the research, people understood and recalled number translations best when the multiplier was 1. For example, "social distance is about the length of a tatami mat" (if you're Japanese) or "almost the length of an adult cassowary" (if you're from Australia), or "approximately an adult gator" (if you don't need your ankles).

Avoid this:	In favor of this:
3.9 times bigger than your home state	About as big as New York's population
1.5 mountain bikes	1 surfboard

Even if "3.9 times your home state" or "1.5 mountain bikes" is more precise, you should favor "New York" and "1 surfboard." They're easier to use and remember, so they are more accurate in practice.

The Republic of Ireland has an area of 70,000 square kilometers. (Yes, we rounded.)	Ireland is half the size of New York State.
Turkey is 783,000 square kilometers.	Turkey is just over twice the size of California.
The Great Pacific Garbage Patch covers an estimated 1.6 million square kilometers.	The Great Pacific Garbage Patch covers an area 3 times the size of Spain.

Okay, now test your skills at creating fathoms. In the Australian summer that bridged 2019 and 2020, wildfires caused unprecedented damage. How could you effectively convey the magnitude of the damage? Choose one of the bulleted translations on the right.

The 2020 Australian wildfires destroyed an estimated 46 million acres, or 186,000 square kilometers.	The 2020 Australian wildfires destroyed an area: • half the size of Japan • as large as Syria • 3/4 the size of the United Kingdom • twice the size of Portugal • as large as New England (Connecticut, Maine, Massachusetts, New Hampshire, Rhode Island, and Vermont) • the size of Washington State

The best number translations blend easily imagined comparisons and simple multipliers. Which of these works best?

Syria isn't well known. England makes us do math. And because our sense of "this is a real thing" kicks in at 1, Japan is out.

For those familiar with it, we like Portugal.

For Americans, Washington State might work for West Coast residents, and New England for the East Coast. (The New England comparison feels bigger since we can visualize each of its ingredients. We'll discuss why this is in the chapter on emotional combos.)

Choosing the right fathom can really help make our messages and numbers more attractive and exciting. Let's look at some scientific facts about speed in the animal kingdom. To help us appreciate how fast wild animals are, we can make our own fathom—our fastest-ever sprinter, Usain Bolt. The fastest person you've ever seen would be put to shame by the average Olympic sprinter, and the average Olympian doesn't get close to the finals. The finalists are the best of the best—and Bolt was strides ahead of all of them when he set his records.

Let's try him against some of nature's average animals—not even the best.

A special cross-species Olympic conference at the Serengeti hammers out the rules for determining the fastest ground species in the 100-meter dash. Each species will be given a running start and can hit the starting line running at top speed. Humans proudly send Usain Bolt, who once recorded an anchor leg of 8.65 seconds in the 4 × 100 m relay. His average speed over 100 meters was 26 mph, or 42 km/h.

—

The chimpanzees send just a random chimp. They have short hind legs and have to run on all fours. Still, the chimp finishes in 8.95 seconds, just 11 feet behind Bolt. They can maintain speeds of 25 mph for 100 meters (40 km/h).

—

But both are put to shame by a black rhino that wandered in at the last minute—they can run up to 34 mph, or 55 km/h, for distances of 100 m. It finishes the race in 6.55 seconds, leaving Bolt 80 feet behind.

—

In a 100-meter race between a black rhino, a chimpanzee, and the greatest sprinter of all time, Usain Bolt would only manage a silver medal—2 seconds behind the rhino. And the animals aren't even sending their best. An ostrich, a cheetah, and—if we allowed flyers—a peregrine falcon would dust the competition.

We can read about how fast animals can run in a science book or on a placard at the zoo, but it doesn't really click until we measure them against our best. The best of our 9 million competitive runners barely beats an average chimpanzee and is nowhere near catching a rhino. And these aren't even the first animals we think of when it comes to running speed.

A truly interesting stat doesn't just convey information, it targets what's counterintuitive. Here's a final example, this one from the business world.

In 2020, the global video games market reached $180 billion. By comparison, in the movie business, world box office revenues were $42 billion in 2019 (pre-COVID), while world music revenues were $22 billion.	The video game industry is more than 4 times the size of the movie industry, and about 9 times the size of the music industry.

Turning the movie industry and the music industry into fathoms helps us measure—and marvel at—the gaming industry in a clear way. Taken one at a time, none of the numbers for video games, movies, or music would seem wild or unexpected. We know all three fields are big business.

But the comparison will likely surprise us. It doesn't match the way we talk about and cover these industries. We hear way less about video games than we do about movies or music. Is there an online *Variety* for video games? Are there Grammys? People's Choice Awards? Perhaps it's geek discrimination; compared with members of the movie and music industries, geeks don't look as good on red carpets.

For the entrepreneurial-minded, this suggests opportunities— there are several Hollywoods' and Nashvilles' worth of economic activity taking place in an industry that's little understood. What do we need to learn in order to tap into that market?

A great fathom gets your audience asking questions. It starts productive conversations about the numbers. And if you can get people talking about your numbers, you have won.

Convert Abstract Numbers into Concrete Objects

Grace Hopper—a computer science pioneer who coined the term "bug" (and who finished her career as *Rear Admiral* Grace Hopper)—was the first head of programming in the U.S. Navy. She also taught math. When students whined about being graded on their writing in a math class, she later remembered, "I would explain: it was no use trying to learn math unless they could communicate with other people."

Hopper pressed her engineers to streamline their code. (In wartime, a fraction of a second can separate life from death.) During lectures, she would hold up a bundle of wire cut to the length that electricity traveled in a microsecond, or 1 one-millionth of a second. It was 984 feet long. She said, "I sometimes think we ought to hang one [of these bundles] over every programmer's desk, or around their neck, so they know what they're throwing away when they throw away microseconds."

"Wasting a microsecond" inspires as little concern as "wasting half a penny" until we *see* how far a signal could have traveled in that time. By turning the microsecond into a concrete object— concrete enough to drape around the neck of a programmer, and make a life-and-death difference in a war—Hopper made an immortal point.

We need to save every "microsecond," which is one-millionth of a second.	This piece of wire is the distance your signal could have traveled in the microsecond you wasted. It stretches 984 feet, about as long as three football fields.

Make Messages Clear by Painting a Picture of Your Number

Hopper was unusual because she was an expert who took the time to talk concretely, in terms that non-experts could understand. It's more common for experts to stay abstract, because that's how they solve problems. They abstract a principle from prior cases and apply it to new dilemmas. Bored with the simple cases, they revel in the complexities. But the rare person who learns to see something complex and make it simple can work at a much larger scale because they allow everyone else to grasp the problem.

There's one easy way to do this: translate your problem from the abstract domain of numbers to the concrete domain of the senses. Concreteness helps us understand faster and remember longer. Cultural products such as proverbs, jokes, folk ballads, and epic sagas become more concrete as they transmit from one person to another, because the concrete parts are more likely to be remembered and passed on.

See how concrete translations make these tumor sizes instantly comprehensible:

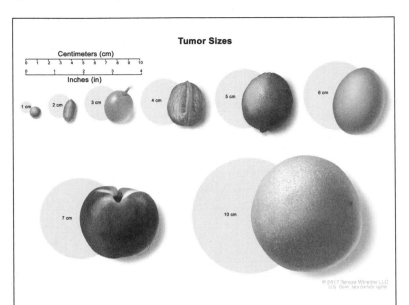

Tumor size	Explanation
1 cm	pea
2 cm	peanut
3 cm	grape
4 cm	walnut
5 cm	lime
6 cm	egg
7 cm	peach
10 cm	grapefruit

It's hard for people to misinterpret or forget a number when their senses are doing the work. Imagine being told, in a hard conversation with a doctor, that your tumor is 3 cm. Half an hour later, you may struggle to remember the number, and may even confuse millimeters and centimeters. But "grape-size" is easy to remember, and hard to confuse. The translations also do the difficult work of converting a measure of length into a three-dimensional object.

These kinds of concrete translations also work for mass or weight. Here's one suggested by the Centers for Disease Control:

The amount of meat recommended as part of a healthy meal is 3 to 4 ounces.	The amount of meat recommended as part of a healthy meal is 3 to 4 ounces, which looks about the same size as a deck of cards.

A deck of playing cards is the same general size across all cultures, no matter whether you play Texas hold'em, Yu-Gi-Oh!, or solitaire. And it's a lot easier to mentally measure a cut of beef against this familiar object than to pull it out of the sauce, shake it off, weigh it, and plop it back on your plate.

Here's one that involves an object that weighs a bit more: The Suez Canal is a geographic shortcut that makes it unnecessary for a ship to travel all the way around the southern tip of Africa to get to Europe from Asia. As a result, a lot of traffic flows through the canal. On March 23, 2021, a container ship, the *Ever Given*, hit a sandstorm that blinded the pilot, resulting in his running the ship aground with such force that the ship was wedged across the canal—taking up so much room that it became impossible for traffic to flow in the shipping channels on either side.

During the crisis, news reporters cast around for ways to explain how a single ship could bring international trade to its knees. Below are two translations.

The container ship *Ever Given* is almost a quarter-mile long.	Imagine the Empire State Building tipped over on its side and blocking the canal. The container ship *Ever Given* is actually longer than the Empire State Building if you take off the tiny, needle-like antenna at the very top of the building.

Concreteness is the first step to making your figures feel real. 3 to 4 ounces is abstract. A deck of cards is concrete. A quarter-mile-long ship is hard to picture. The Empire State Building tipped over and blocking a canal is an image you'll carry for a long time.

The last image suggests that there is room to go past just making things concrete. You could make "a quarter mile" concrete by translating it into "5 north-south blocks in Manhattan." But you go beyond a simple concrete image when you ask people to imagine the famously vertical Empire State building (which reigned for almost 40 years in a row as the world's tallest structure) tipped over and lying on its side to block the canal. That image is substantially more vivid. If you're aiming for a deeper impact, you can go beyond concreteness to vividness. Vivid messages are more sensory, more colorful, more active, more surprising, and are closer to *you*. You don't just understand them, you feel them.

Many citizens dislike the food stamp program (now called

SNAP: Supplemental Nutrition Assistance Program) because it seems like an expensive, perhaps even extravagant, free lunch. The total amount of the subsidy sounds massive—$61 billion in 2018. But if we break that number down to the amount received per person per meal (yes, recall the chapter on "focus on 1"), the average is only $1.37. Thinking of a dollar and assorted change makes concrete the small size of the "free lunch," but translating it into meals makes the experience vivid.

The average amount allocated by SNAP per person, per meal, is only $1.37.	From a website advertising recipes under $1.50 per serving, we get suggestions such as 1 serving of tomato-macaroni salad ($1.41 per serving), 1 of potato leek soup ($1.28 per serving), or almost 3 of crunchy tuna casserole (50 cents per serving).

Whether or not those sound like must-have recipes, the dishes are in no way luxurious. There is nothing to strike envy in the heart of a SNAP-skeptical voter. And even these humble dishes may be out of reach for SNAP participants—what the recipe writers don't tell you is that, while the recipes may cost only $1.50 per serving for the food you consume during that meal, to hit the $1.50 price point, you'd better already have a well-stocked pantry and spice rack. For example, the crunchy tuna recipe depends on 3 tablespoons of butter, which is sold by the pound for around $3.00 at Walmart—that's almost the SNAP allowance for a full day.

Here's another example of turning the concrete into the vivid:

The wealthiest 1% of Americans own 31% of the wealth in the country. The top 10% own around 70%. And the bottom half own just 2%.	Imagine an apartment building with 10 units on each floor and 100 in total. The richest person owns 31 apartments. Together the 10 wealthiest people in the building own 70 of the apartments. The poorest person shares ownership with everyone who is worth less than $100,000. If that's you, then you and 49 others would share 2 apartments.

You might think this concrete visual would lend itself to an infographic, and you wouldn't be wrong, but the brain is a high-tech graphics processor on its own. We can build a three-dimensional image of this apartment with our imagination (our apartment building has brown bricks like the one Chandler and Joey and Monica and Rachel lived in). And our brain versions are more compelling than any infographic, because we can feel the vivid sensation of being crowded in 2 small apartments with 49 other people—no infographic has ever made people feel claustrophobic.

Vivid translations can conjure other senses as well. This concrete imagining of what it might be like to be a hummingbird works with the sense of taste and bodily feeling:

Hummingbirds weigh about 3 grams and consume between 3 and 7 calories a day, making their metabolism nearly 50 times faster than humans.	A hummingbird's metabolism is so fast that, if it were the size of an average adult human male, it would need to consume slightly more than a Coke every waking minute—67 cokes an hour, for 16 hours a day.

We don't immediately have a sense of what a faster metabolism means, especially with a multiplier like "50 times." But imagining drinking a Coke every minute makes the figure both concrete (we can translate it to material food) and vivid (we can imagine the sugar buzz, overwhelming after minutes and just keeps building all day—no wonder hummingbirds move their wings so fast!). Instead of feeling like we're reading a biology textbook, we're expanding our sense of wonder.

In general, vivid things are more colorful and more active; they are more immediate—something is happening now, happening here, and happening to us. All of these things make a situation more memorable and more likely to motivate us to change how we act and think.

When something's in our personal space, it feels vivid, especially if there's also a familiar action involved:

One Saturday in 2014, in Toledo, Ohio (metro population, 650,000), municipal officials asked the 500,000 people served by the metropolitan area's water system to stop using tap water after toxins from algae were found at a regional water treatment plant.	Of the 650,000 residents of the Toledo, Ohio metro area, 4 out of 5 households can't fill up a glass from the kitchen faucet in their own home and drink the water without swallowing toxins from algae.

Toxins at a treatment plant are a news story. Toxins in your tap are a personal threat. This translation brings the problem to where it impacts people's lives. We've all filled up a glass of water—we can imagine how it would feel if that simple act were deadly.

We started this chapter with the esoteric: the length of a microsecond. We have no illusions about actually understanding a microsecond on its own. We embrace the value of concreteness here because it's clearly telling us something we don't know. Hopper's translation is something we can grasp.

Similarly, the distances in the following translation are hard to conceive and we know it:

The distance to the nearest solar system is 4.25 light-years.	How far away is the nearest star from us? Well, imagine shrinking the solar system down to the size of a quarter. You leave a quarter at the goalpost of a soccer field and walk toward the goalpost at the other end of the field. When you reach it, drop another quarter to represent the solar system of our nearest neighbor, Proxima Centauri. Everything between the quarters is just cold, dark space.

The focus here is the vastness of space, which is best conjured in concrete terms as a distance to be traveled. If you put it all in the span of a room, or a single large canvas, it would just be something to be viewed—nowhere near as powerful.

The speed of electrons in a nanosecond, the vastness of space as measured in light-years. We recognize that we need tools to help us with these. But numbers are so foreign to us at a gut level that even the simplest numbers stand to benefit from concrete translation. We think we know what 7 years means. But we don't really. Anything that puts a number in context magnifies the impact of that number.

Chip's students taught him a lesson in concreteness a few years back when he challenged them to come up with a way of helping consumers understand the advantages of carbon fluorescent light-bulbs (CFLs). At the time, they cost more than traditional incandescent bulbs (around $7 compared with $1), but they used only a quarter of the electricity. When it was time for students to report, one group said that they had taken the liberty of altering Chip's assignment based on his own principles. "Electricity consumption is fundamentally abstract," they said, "so we decided to focus on ease of replacement. These bulbs are expected to last for 7 years; that's way better than replacing bulbs every year, particularly for those hard-to-get-to sockets." Their message is below on the right.

CFLs use a quarter of the electricity of standard bulbs and last for 7 years in between replacements compared with the "replace every year" cycle for typical bulbs.	Replace your lights with CFLs when your child is learning how to walk. The next time you'd have to replace the bulb, your child would be in second grade, learning about oxygen. The next time, they'd be taking driver's ed.

This was one of the few times in a teaching career of over 20 years when Chip heard his students applaud a classmate's answer. He clapped, too.

7 years seems simple. But the passage of time is a hard concept to grasp in passing. In real life, it often flies past us and only becomes noticeable when we focus on vivid life milestones. Once we do, we not only understand it, we truly feel it: Wow, that's one long-lasting lightbulb! (But also: *My time with my kids is short! Better arrange that zoo trip for next weekend!*)

Chip learned two things from this exercise: 1) If students want to challenge themselves, let them. 2) Even something as simple and concrete as "7 years" can benefit from more concreteness.

Here's one last example of how concreteness can add poignancy. (There are many variants of this meme on the web; we've fact-checked this one for you.)

Imagine if Earth's 7.7 billion people were shrunk to a village of 100:

>> *26 villagers would be children (14 years old or younger). 5 villagers would come from North America, 8 from Latin America, 10 from Europe, 17 from Africa, and 60 from Asia.*

>> *31 would be Christians, 24 Muslims, 15 Hindus, and 7 Buddhists. 7 villagers would represent every other religion, and 16 wouldn't identify with a religion.*

>> *7 people would speak English as a first language, and another 20 would speak it as a second. 14 villagers would be illiterate; 7 would have a college degree.*

>> *29 people would be overweight, and 10 would be going hungry.*

The original stat here is a large table of demographic statistics—too long to even put in the text as a side-by-side. It's the kind of thing that few people would read on their own.

But these are all stats about people, and the concrete way to express them is in terms of people. Once you start to imagine people, not as billions, too many to count or meet, but as real inhabitants of a community that you're in, the number really sinks in. It's not a model of one particular problem, but it helps you rethink your idea of what kinds of people exist in the world, whether you're drafting a global policy or a marketing plan.

No matter how developed our mathematical tool kits may be, they will never be as instinctive as our tool kits for thinking of concrete problems. Use your mind's strength as a strength; make your numbers concrete.

Recast Your Number in Different Dimensions: Try Time, Space, Distance, Money, and Pringles

If your car is going 30 miles per hour, that trip feels like a normal ride through the neighborhood. If it's 30 feet long, it's a stretch limo. If it's 30 pounds, it's a toy. If it's 30 degrees inside its temperature-controlled cabin, it's too cold (Fahrenheit) or too hot (Celsius). There's no feeling attached to "30" itself—every unit you could apply it to measures a different experience, and different experiences are handled by different parts of your brain.

You can take advantage of this to understand numbers. If a number, calculation, or comparison doesn't make immediate sense, try converting it to a whole other type of quantity—distance, volume, density, speed, temperature, money, time—and see if you can understand it better.

Converting to time is useful in many situations because, in a world ruled by schedules, we have plenty of experience clocking it. We might not know how many kilometers away our favorite coffee spot is, but we know just how long it takes to get there.

Notice in the next example how simply converting an abstract number to time makes the number feel more real—because now we're talking about our lives.

A million seconds is 12 days.	A billion is 1,000 times greater than 1,000,000.	A billion seconds is 32 years.

Try making these conversions in every dimension. Let's say you're multiplying something by 300. What does that mean? If you multiply the average height of an American (5'6") by 300, the person becomes taller than the Eiffel Tower with the Statue of Liberty on top. It means that instead of walking from 34th Street in Manhattan to Central Park, you could walk all the way to Montreal. "This will take just a minute" means a 5-hour delay (which happens in airports every day). A $5 bill becomes $1,500. An elevator ride with your boss actually lasts 10 hours, instead of just feeling like it.

All of these things are more visceral, in different ways, than the simple operation "times 300." Each has its advantage. Think of this chapter as inspiration—a set of trades to have in your repertoire, rather than a strict set of rules.

See if you can master each trade:

Trade Time for Money

Our development team of 100 engineers drinks a lot of coffee . . . Equipping each floor with new coffee stations would cost $15,000, plus additional ongoing fees for supplies and maintenance.

At 10 minutes a day per person traveling down to the break room for coffee and back, our engineering department spends 80 hours a week getting caffeine. New coffee makers would pay for themselves within weeks; afterward, they'd make money *for* the company.

Our current system acts as if we've hired 2 full-time engineers just to walk back and forth from their offices to the break room, and their hall banter isn't even close to *West Wing* quality.

Express Probability in Terms of Things You Can Count

There are a little more than 50 million people in England, and around 50 deaths each day via accidental causes (slipping in the tub; being swept away in a flooding river; falling from a ladder). The daily risk of dying there in an accident is roughly 1 in a million.	Your risk of dying unexpectedly in England on any given day is the same as your odds of having to guess which date someone is thinking of between 500 BC and August 1, 2200.

The 1-in-a-million chance of accidental death described above was explored by researchers who were interested in creating a baseline and a unit to measure all types of risk. They called this 1-in-a-million unit a "micromort" and started collecting data to locate various risks on the micromort scale. Riding a motorcycle 44 miles a day (11 micromorts). Undergoing general anesthesia (5 micromorts). Skydiving, one jump (7 micromorts). But this equates the empirical rates of death from various risks; it doesn't help people feel the risks involved.

We have a proposal for a universal measure of probability—based not on micromorts but Hogwarts. Imagine the entire Harry Potter series shelved in a library. Take the second volume, *Harry Potter and the Chamber of Secrets* off the shelf (it's always been your favorite), and you're left with 6 books, which together have approximately 1,000,000 words of text . . . Now, pick one of the remaining volumes, open it to a random page, and draw a red *X* over a random word. Then replace that volume, and take the *Chamber of Secrets* with you to read in the cafe.

Now if someone else entered the library and, without looking, picked a page in one of the volumes and put their finger down on a word, the chance of them picking the word with your red X is 1 in a million.

The Harry Potter metric can be extended to think about other probabilities. For example, as mentioned above, the chance of dying in a skydiving accident is 7 micromorts—roughly 7 in a million—so ask a friend to go cross out 7 words across all the volumes. In this case, the Harry Potter analogy helps us be braver. We're more scared when we hear "7 in a million," because our attention is drawn to the unfortunate 7 who didn't make it, as opposed to the 999,993 who had a bucket-list moment. Picturing only 7 red Xs in thousands of pages helps us look at the risk in a less fearful way.

| Odds of winning Powerball: 1 in 292,201,338 | Imagine having to guess which *second* of a day someone is thinking of—any date, hour, minute, and second from the time they're born to the time they turn 9. If you match, you win the lottery prize. | The jackpot is yours. All you have to do is think of the resident of the United States whose name is written down over there on that folded piece of paper. (Hint: they are older than the age of 10.) |

Convert Abstract Numbers into Counts of Objects

Think of objects made of many component parts: bricks in a building, drops in a bathtub, words in a book, steps in a journey.

| In 2016, the $148 million allocated to the National Endowment for the Arts accounted for .004% of the federal budget expenditures ($3.9 trillion). Suppose we eliminated it in response to criticism? | Trying to balance the budget by eliminating the NEA would be like editing a 90,000-word novel by eliminating 4 words. |

Convert Calories to Well-Understood Actions

A single M&M has 4 calories.	In order to burn off the calories in a single M&M, you'd have to walk 2 flights of stairs.
A single Pringle has 10 calories.	In order to burn off the calories in a single Pringle, you'd have to walk 176 yards, or almost 2 football fields.

Convert Status to a Vertical Everyone Can Understand

Her paper is in the top 100 most-cited papers in Web of Science.
"The colossal size of the scholarly literature means that the top 100 papers are extreme outliers. Web of Science holds some 58 million items. If that corpus were scaled to Mount Kilimanjaro, then the 100 most-cited papers would represent just 1 centimeter at the peak. Only 14,499 papers—roughly a meter and a half's worth—have more than 1,000 citations. Meanwhile, the foothills comprise works that have been cited only once, if at all—a group that encompasses roughly half of the items." —from Nature.com

Now that we've seen an array of these interdimensional transla-tions, let's take a moment to appreciate the versatility of numbers. If we heard that an alien species had a word that could be meaning-fully used to describe things as varied as the height of mountains, the speed of travel, the difficulty of games, the nutritional content of food, the reaction in a moment, the way we plan our day, the passage of a lifetime, and our relative success at publishing, we'd be in awe of their linguistic flexibility. But numbers actually can do all these things.

Even people who work with numbers regularly forget this. We might want to let numbers speak for themselves, but to leave num-bers on their own is selling short their unique flexibility. Whenever possible, we should take advantage of the amazing power numbers have to describe any dimension of our experience and still make sense.

Whether you're trying to explain a number or trying to compre-hend it for yourself, remember that power. Here's an exercise for you: How many ways can you make sense of 1%? This is a number we see so often we forget that we might not have an intuitive sense of it. How would you translate it? What dimension would you use? Here are a couple of examples.

>> It's one penny out of a dollar.
>> It's one year in a century.

Give yourself two minutes to come up with others and then take a look at what we came up with.*

A Bad Example of Mixing Your Measurements

Speaking to Congress in February 1981, Ronald Reagan used this example to explain the national debt, which for the first time in history was nearing $1 trillion:

> *"If you had a stack of thousand-dollar bills in your hand only 4 inches high, you'd be a millionaire. A trillion dollars would be a stack of thousand-dollar bills 67 miles high."*

Reagan, known as a brilliant and charismatic communicator, was trying to convince Americans that the national debt was too high. Behind Reagan in the effort was a team of political scientists, policy wonks, and speechwriters—a team of the most articulate people in the nation—trying to urgently persuade the American public on an issue meaningful to the conservative principles they valued—which certainly didn't involve going into debt to finance a government sector that was way too large. They had the bulliest pulpit in the world, cross-network exposure on the Big Three networks in the country, and, with most Americans' eyes riveted to the television . . . they chose to stack currency.

When was the last time you scrutinized a price by stacking dollar bills? And when was the last time you saw a sign at the market that read: "Avocados—a stack of nickels 3.07 inches tall"? (Yes, we fact-checked the number in the joke.[†] Yes, we are geeks.)

"67 miles high" is abstract. The size of the debt is still a mystery. What else could he have done to make this amount clear?

---

[*]   Translating 1%: Ways to feel/sense/understand 1%: It's 1 Pringle in a can of 100. It's 1 card between 2 decks. It's 4 days out of the year. It's 1 meter in a 100-meter dash. It's one minute out of an average-length movie.

[†]   The average avocado is about $2, and nickels are 1.95mm thick. Forty nickels × 1.95 mm = 78 mm tall. Divided by 25.4 mm per inch = 3.07 inches.

What if Reagan had used the power of 1 instead, and said that every man, woman, and child in the United States owed $4,000 or—probably more useful—if he had grouped people and said that every household owed about $12,000?

Things would have been a lot clearer, though probably less scary. Most families owed more than that on their mortgage. The median home in 1984 was selling for $80,000. If people put down 20% and financed the rest, the typical household would have $64,000 of mortgage debt.

We can argue about whether or not being less scary suited Reagan's purposes, but treating the number as an obligation per household rather than a fragile column of stacked bills likely would have helped spur a bipartisan discussion on the debt.

When we come to a number, we should bring our intuition to bear. Intuition often helps us clarify more abstract dimensions. We "get" the difference between millions and billions when we translate both to seconds, and we understand the concept of light-years better when we pace off distances on a soccer field. Choosing arbitrary metrics is not always an improvement; stacking a trillion dollars of cash didn't help us have a productive discussion of the national debt. But a wisely chosen translation into a useful or relevant dimension may change the way we think or act. Picturing the odds of tragedy from skydiving as 7 words crossed out in the million-word Harry Potter epic has us thinking skydiving might be next up on our bucket list. We know number translations are powerful when they can make us feel brave enough to jump out of a high-flying plane.

Human Scale: Use the Goldilocks Principle to Make Your Numbers Just Right

We just showed you an example of a bad comparison—a trillion dollars to a stack of bills that reached the top layer of Earth's atmosphere, something nobody could really envision because it had no place in their world.

Some things are too vast to fathom—like the distance to the sun, the volume of the ocean, and the height of Mount Everest. Other things are too small—nanoparticles, or viruses, or our chances of getting tickets to a BTS concert. In order to understand dimensions that are larger and smaller than our experience, we need to translate them to human scale.

How would we make sense of the size of Mount Everest, as compared to other mountains? Let's imagine ourselves to be very small, but still visible, so we don't lose track.

The middle translation, shrinking humans down to pencil-eraser size, winds up with Everest the size of a 7-1/2-story building. The building doesn't have many comparisons in day-to-day experience; it's too short for city dwellers and too tall for suburbanites.

Mount Everest is 29,000 feet high.	If we were the height of a pencil eraser, Mount Everest would be a 7-1/2-story building.	If we were the height of 6 playing cards stacked flat, Everest in comparison would be about the size of a suburban two-story house with an attic.

In the translation on the far right, we get closer to many people's experience. If humans shrink to the size of a stack of six playing cards (which conveniently puts us on an easy-to-convert 1,000-to-1 scale), Mount Everest would be a 29-foot building, like a suburban two-story home. The world's second-highest mountain, K2, would be 28 feet, 3 inches—only 9 inches short of Everest.

Having the right comparison starts to put things in perspective and generate some insights. We can imagine the stack of cards dwarfed by these imposing buildings. But what may have surprised you is that K2 is so close to the height of Everest. And it's not alone. It's called K2, or Karakoram 2, because there are so many giant mountains in the area that scientists didn't even bother to name them. (Karakoram is the name of the range.) The Himalayas combined have over 100 peaks over 23,000 feet, or 23 feet in our scale model. Together, these peaks dwarf the rest of the world.

In fact, the Himalayas have a head start: they sit on the Tibetan plateau, which averages 14,800 feet—and that's the top of the "foothills."

So imagine high-mountain Asia as a neighborhood, spanning several city blocks. The buildings (mountains) are 23 to 29 feet high, with Everest at the highest. They share a courtyard patio, the Tibetan plateau, that is 14 feet, 10 inches off the ground.

How does that mountain range compare to other neighborhoods? The tallest of the Rocky Mountains is 14 feet, 5 inches, not even the height of the patio. Mont Blanc, the tallest of the Alps, at 15 feet, 9 inches would at least peek above the Tibetan patio by approximately a foot. The Appalachians top out at 6 feet, 11 inches, low enough that the average person can reach up and touch the top of them. Scotland's so-called Highlands stands 4 foot 5 at best. Still tall compared to a short stack of cards, but no comparison to the highest peaks in the world.

It took a while to set up, but that simple transformation gave us a fairly deep look at the world's geography, something that never quite clicked from decades of casually absorbing atlas figures or even from explicit instruction in school. It just took the right scale. If we'd made the mountains too large, they'd have all seemed unapproachable. Too small, and we lose an appreciation for their variations—plus the human, that stack of 6 cards, is no longer on the map.

For a good human-scale comparison, make use of the clarity of common everyday items. Use things that are concrete and familiar:

Recall these facts from earlier: Just 2.5% of the world's water is unsalty, and over 99% of that is trapped in glaciers and snowfields. Only .025% of water is actually drinkable by humans and animals.

If the world's water were put into an Olympic-size pool, humans would only be able to drink 46 gallons of it—roughly the amount that can be contained in a standard bathtub.	If the world's water were put into a gallon jug, humans would only be able to drink less than 20 drops of it.

Both the pool and the gallon jug comparisons are better than the list of percentages.

But while the Olympic-size pool makes things concrete, it's still not familiar. We may have seen one, in person or on TV, but we don't have an immediate sense of how much water goes into one of those things.

As we have seen people use measurements like "Olympic-size pool," "elephants," and "jumbo jets" because of a bias we call big-ism—the instinct to go for large, seemingly impressive comparisons. Big-ism wows our senses, but it doesn't cultivate understanding. After a certain point, we're just saying, "*Whoa.*"

In our Everest example, we went in the opposite direction, taking imposing mountains and making them into medium-size houses. That's the power of human scale. For all our lives, we'd been able to look at mountains and say, "Whoa" . . . but now we can say, "Oh, I get it."

Besides being the wrong scale, big-ism leads us to unfamiliar experiences. We've never filled an Olympic-size pool, and we've hopefully never drunk from a bathtub. We can't match these things to our memories.

But look at that second example, with the gallon jug. We've filled a gallon jug before, and we've had a few drops of water. The comparison on the right puts it in terms you can easily imagine, without having to imagine the taste of chlorine.

Here's another example of how ordinary objects beat big-ism, and make a complex feat even more impressive. The illustration below is found in Jeffrey Kluger's *Apollo 8: The Thrilling Story of the First Mission to the Moon.*

In order to enter the atmosphere safely, the crew of Apollo 8 had to aim for a window of entry just over 2 degrees wide.

Place a baseball and a basketball 23 feet apart—about the distance of a 3-point line from the basket. Get some paper:

"If the Earth were the size of a basketball and the moon were the

size of a baseball, the two worlds would be positioned twenty-three feet apart and the fifteen-mile-wide reentry corridor would be no thicker than a piece of paper."

Finding the right scale in this example isn't easy. There are 4 essential measurements—the size of Earth, the size of the moon, the space between them, and the paper-thin reentry window. But with the right focus, all 4 can be human scale at the same time. If we tried to increase the thickness of the reentry window (say, to represent it with a credit card) the distance between the moon and Earth would be too big to fit in any normal room. This simple illustration—easy to understand, not too hard to actually create—makes us appreciate the difficulty of NASA's task, in a world in which the most common computing device was a slide rule, to take precise actions like reentry with only low-tech ingenuity.

Just as we shrink down vast quantities, we can magnify small ones. We're amazed by the navigational capabilities of the desert ant, as illustrated by the writers of this book on navigation in the natural world.

"Desert ants search for food at distances of up to hundreds of meters from their nest, covering a radius that would be equivalent, in human terms, to about 38 kilometers. Yet these ants, once they find food, can plot a direct course back to their nest and find it within 1 square centimeter of error."	". . . covering a radius that would be equivalent, in human terms, to about 38 kilometers"—bigger than the urban DC metro area, from the National Institutes of Health in Maryland, to the Pentagon in Virginia. "Yet these ants, once they find food, can plot a direct course back to their nest and find it within 1 square centimeter of error"—about the size of an M&M.

It's hard to fathom how far these ants are wandering in search of food, until we bring them up to our size. Once we do, and discover that they wander a region equivalent to the metro Washington, DC, area, we can fully appreciate their outstanding navigation system. Imagine wandering past the Capitol, the Washington Monument, the White House, out past the international embassies in one direction and the Pentagon in another, and knowing at every moment which direction to turn and walk a straight line back to your hotel room. Google Maps would be less useful.

Here's another magnification, this one in the dimension of time. The difference between the speed of light and sound is almost imperceptible to us—the interval between them is just too quick. But what if we slow them down, and stretch the amount of time they take to reach us?

Light travels 186,000 miles per second. Sound travels 760 miles per hour.

Imagine counting down on New Year's Eve to a gigantic fireworks display that you know was going to be set off at midnight on January 1. You eagerly start watching at midnight, and at 10 seconds after midnight, the light from the fireworks arrives. It's massive—easily the largest display you've ever seen.

Question: How long would it take the sound to reach you (assuming the laws of physics would allow you to hear it)?

Answer: If it took 10 seconds for the light to reach you, then the sound wouldn't arrive until April 12, just in time for people to mistake it as the beginning of an unusually vicious April shower that will bring May flowers.

This magnification puts both quantities at human scale. We had to think for a while to choose a starting point that would connect the light and sound so that both "10 seconds" and "more than 3-1/2 months" were in focus, but New Year's Eve did the trick. We count down the seconds until the New Year, then start counting the days, weeks, and months since.

Financial differences could also benefit from magnification.

According to researchers at Northwestern University, Black families with kids have a single penny in wealth for every dollar held by White families with kids.	Consider two thought experiments to make clear the implications of the penny/dollar discrepancy: Imagine a child breaking a leg, racking up $1,500 in doctors' bills. If a typical White family has $2,000 in a checking account, a Black family has only $20. Imagine reaching retirement age: a White family has $500,000. A Black family would have $5,000—and probably find it impossible to retire.

Comparisons like this are apt to slip by us because we're so used to seeing phrases like "pennies on the dollar." The problem is, we don't notice the difference between a penny and a dollar. Neither pays for anything life-changing. Even though both seem human-scale, they don't have human-scale financial impacts.

Instead of looking at pennies and dollars, we can bring this into human scale by comparing situations where wealth really comes into play. The difference between having enough to pay for an ER visit and not having it is huge; so is the difference between having enough to retire, and just enough to survive the next few months.

Examples like the above are relatively straightforward to magnify because we're dealing with a ratio—one penny to one dollar. Ratios are made to scale up and down. Other times, we need to do something a little different to bring small quantities into human scale. We have to add them up until they become noticeable.

A study of exemplary teachers found that they spent a surprising amount of time thinking about logistics. Effective high-school math teachers began the class with a "Do Now" problem written on the board when students entered the classroom (for example, find a proof that angle A is equal to angle F). The teacher would plunge into discussing the Do Now as soon as the start bell rang, so students learned to finish before class started.

How would you convince teachers to adopt the Do Now practice?

"For each class you assign a Do Now, you gain an extra 5 minutes of discussion time."	"Over a year, adding 5 minutes per class is equivalent to adding 3 weeks to the school year. Think of how many cool demonstrations or interesting topics you could add with another 3 weeks to play with."

From a teacher's point of view, an extra 5 minutes of discussion time may not seem like a lot. Some teachers may not imagine much that they can do in that time, and may not do the extra work to prepare additional material. But if it ends up buying 3 weeks of classroom time over the course of the year, that's a real, tangible result that any passionate teacher can appreciate. 3 extra weeks actually does mean a lot more time to teach what you care about, and a lot less stress meeting deadlines. If that's possible with one simple practice, it's easily worth doing.

Here's another example you can apply whether or not you have a classroom:

The average American spends 2 hours a day on social media.

vs.

Suppose you were willing to give up your 2 hours of Facebook on Fridays. Well, 5 months from today, you could say that you've made it all the way through War and Peace. *And all you have to do is give up Facebook on Fridays.*

Again, the intervention doesn't seem hard. It's only one day a week, not giving up cold turkey. But an extra 2 hours won't change your life, especially if you don't feel like you have the energy to work or exercise.

Over time, however, a simple human-scale change, reading a book instead of a Facebook feed, can add up to a real human-scale achievement. Here are some of the things you could accomplish in five months of Fridays: 1) read *War and Peace*: impress your Russian friends and neighbors, never have to buy a vodka shot again, never want to take a vodka shot again; 2) read the entire *Lord of the Rings* trilogy: establish your geek cred, consider the art of creating worlds from the master of it, learn to speak a little Elvish; 3) read half of the *Encyclopedia Britannica*'s list of "Greatest Book[s] Ever Written"—including *The Great Gatsby, Jane Eyre, The Color Purple,* and *Things Fall Apart.*

All of these are the kinds of activities that would lead to interesting conversations the next time you see your friends (your offline friends, the ones you can touch—post-vaccination). None of these would be the biggest achievement of your life—nothing on the scale of learning Mandarin, mastering physics, or becoming a working mechanic. But they are the kind of significant adult learning milestones that makes you pay attention.

Whether we're shrinking down mountains or adding up moments, human scale helps us understand things more fully by bringing us into a realm of experience where we're hyper-trained to notice things. It's obvious when something ridiculously huge or tiny—telescopic or microscopic—is outside of human scale, but there are many things just on the boundaries of our experience that are still outside our full understanding.

Before we promoted the navigational achievements of the desert ant to human scale, we might admire the foraging runs of the ants at hundreds of meters, but it's a very abstract kind of admiration. We comprehend more and we feel more when things are human-size. At our scale, our vague admiration for the desert ant turns to deep respect. By all rights, the desert ant should be written into the annals of the best navigators of all time (alongside Magellan and London taxi drivers). If your number is not being taken seriously enough, try shrinking or growing it to human scale.

USE EMOTIONAL
NUMBERS—SURPRISING
AND MEANINGFUL—
TO MOVE PEOPLE
TO THINK AND ACT
DIFFERENTLY

Florence Nightingale Avoids Dry Statistics by Using Transferred Emotion

In 1850s Britain, in the aftermath of the Crimean War, a new type of hero had emerged. On a strategic level, the war had been a success, as the UK worked with an alliance of European and Turkish forces to decisively deter the Russian invasion. But for the British troops, the war had been a disaster, especially in the military hospitals, where troops were being ravaged by infection and neglect. Candid foreign reporting brought this reality to the home front. In 1855, in the middle of the war, *The Times* of London wrote, "there is not even linen to make bandages for the wounded," who are "left to expire in agony."

The hero who saved the troops from this fate was not a general but a 34-year-old administrator named Florence Nightingale, who before the war worked at the Institution for the Care of Sick Gentlewomen in Distressed Circumstances. Nightingale had grown up wealthy, determined, and intellectually curious, pushing for a broad and serious education beyond the art and music usually allowed to women in her class. She read obsessively, tutored with her father in math, science, and classics, and studied medicine at Kaiserswerther Diakonie, a hospital and training center for Lutheran deaconesses.

In 1854, Nightingale proposed to the army that she go to the frontlines of the war to help in the hospitals, along with a brigade of 38 volunteer nurses she'd personally recruited. Arriving in Turkey, they discovered squalor. Inside the hospitals, rats ran rampant, and bloody bandages stayed on soldiers for days. What little food the soldiers received was often moldy, rotten, or rancid.

Working 20-hour days, Nightingale turned the situation around. She ate standing up. She begged people at home to send clean towels. She organized all the equipment at the hospital and installed routines to ensure that the food provided by suppliers was unspoiled and healthy. She collected data throughout. By the end of the war, she had not only reorganized the hospital system at the front—dramatically reducing the casualty rates in the second half of the war—but she had become a national hero, her efforts heralded in the national press.

Although she returned beloved and celebrated, Nightingale saw her mission extending beyond the Crimean War. She figured, correctly, that without substantial reform, the same disorganization that had cost so many lives on the battlefront would continue to cost lives. She had the clout to gain audiences with both the queen and military leaders and had statistics to back up her argument. But she still faced an uphill battle. She needed to convince high-ranking, change-averse people—military officers, doctors, lords, and nobles—that they could not return to business as usual, even after the end of a long campaign.

The numbers spoke to people like Nightingale and her friend the physician and statistician William Farr, who understood the language of numbers fluently. In fact, in a letter to Farr, Nightingale chided Farr for complaining that he had written a boring statistical report. "You complain that your report would be dry. The dryer the better. Statistics should be the driest of all reading." But when it came time to spread her arguments more broadly, she did not, in fact, leave the statistics in dry form. Her use of statistics in her letters, articles, and testimonies are vivid and compelling—as well as innovative.

But Nightingale was aware that things didn't happen just because people understood the numbers. The numbers needed to be translated into a form that would motivate critical actors to take action, overcoming the inertia in the system, overturning the policies that had led to the disaster in the Crimean War. The numbers needed to be translated into a more potent, more emotional form that would spur people to act.

Ahead of her peers—by more than a century—she started by equating basket size.

In its first 7 months, 7,857 troops died out of 13,095.	Nightingale's translation: We had 600 deaths per 1,000 troops.

Principle: measure in small, equal baskets.

Nightingale first cut down the figure to something that could compare neatly to other causes. You'll recall that we recommended small baskets. "Out of every 5 soldiers, 3 would die" might make this more visceral to average people.

But we also said to use numbers your audience was familiar with, and military commanders and policy makers are used to making decisions that affect large numbers of people. Besides, the count was just a stat along her way to the core of her method, finding an analogy that she could compare to, one that was also likely measured in large numbers.

She made sure she found a comparison that would resonate emotionally.

Statistical translation: We had 600 deaths per 1,000 troops.	Nightingale's translation: "We had, in the first seven months of the Crimean campaign . . . from disease alone, a rate of mortality which exceeds that of the Great Plague of London."

Principle: uses a "comparative" (see next chapter) that is especially vivid by virtue of a proximal location.

The Great Plague, a euphemism for the Black Death or bubonic plague, would have been unforgettable to Londoners—it was the most famous plague in Britain's history.

In army hospitals, 25–35-year-old British soldiers in peacetime had mortality rates of around 19 per 1,000, compared with 11 per 1,000 in London hospitals.	Nightingale's translation: "It is as criminal to have a mortality of . . . 19 . . . per 1,000 in the Line, Artillery and Guards in England, when that of Civil life is only 11 per 1,000, as it would be to take 1,100 men per annum out upon Salisbury Plain and shoot them."

Principle: make numbers concrete and vivid. Lining up our soldiers and shooting them is as vivid as it gets (contrast the lack of urgency you feel when you think about passively "losing" a soldier to an acquired infection).

The "1,100" comes from the peacetime death rate of soldiers multiplied by the size of the enlisted force. Salisbury Plain is not a foreign battlefield but a drill field in England—you've seen it in the background of its most famous landmark, Stonehenge. By staging the "execution" there, she made the statistic vivid as well as concrete—active slaughter not on the battlefield in some foreign country but on the parade field typically used to show Britain's military might.

She used a comparison to an event her audience already knew:

We are losing 1,100 men per year to preventable causes!

Nightingale's translation: "We hear with horror of the loss of 400 men onboard the *Birkenhead* by carelessness at sea; but what should we feel if we were told that 1,100 men are annually doomed to death in our Army at home by causes which might be prevented?"

Principle: see the next chapter on comparatives. The *Birkenhead* is a story that has preexisting pools of emotion (anger, sadness).

The *Birkenhead* was the *Titanic* of the mid-19th century, a supposedly unsinkable ship that met with disaster. The 400 soldiers on the ship gallantly shuttled the women and children onto the lifeboats and then drowned when the capacity ran out. The event is credited as the origin of the phrase "women and children first," though there is no record of that phrase being uttered during that event. Nightingale doesn't make the scale, almost three *Birkenhead*s a year, explicit, but she doesn't need to. "Worse than the *Birkenhead*" says enough to the audience of the time.

Her vivid, passionate, dramatic, un-dry statistics worked, making sure the systemic problems she'd painstakingly measured made it through to Britain's top brass.

Nightingale is an adept curator of emotional energy—think of the different sources of emotion she taps into and channels to suit her purposes. She tackles the history of plagues in England. She channels the then-current, "ripped from the headlines" tragedy of the *Birkenhead*. She anticipates modern debates in moral philosophy about the morality of losing lives through an act of commission versus passive neglect, asking the military establishment why we are allowing 1,100 soldiers to die every year for lack of simple acts of sanitation, when we would never agree to gun them down on the parade field at Salisbury (which the soldiers might have preferred because it would have saved them the misery of suffering before they die with a body-wasting disease).

After the British military adopted Nightingale's ideas, disease and mortality declined; the average hospital stay shrank. The army had "planned hospital beds for 10% of its force, but with the sanitary reforms made after the war beds for only 5–6% were needed." Responding to the news that the army was realizing they had overbuilt, Nightingale quipped with tongue firmly in cheek: "Really it is not our fault if the number of sick has fallen so much that they can't fill their hospitals."

Nightingale achieved the impossible: As a woman in Victorian England, without title, elected position, military rank, or medical degree, she convinced the lords and doctors and generals to see the world in a different way.

One historian wrote an article on Florence Nightingale called "The Compassionate Statistician" and made the case that she never forgot the horror of men suffering in the hospital. She felt a connection to those soldiers for the rest of her life.

But when it came time to convince others to feel that way, Nightingale did not just tell her own emotional story. That's a common trap. Many storytellers relay their experiences and assume that others will feel the same emotional connection to the subject matter. It's like a personal version of the curse of knowledge—forgetting that your own relationship to the subject is forged by personal experience that the audience may not share. Some audiences may even discredit storytellers with personal stories because they assume that an "emotional" storyteller lacks objectivity.

Nightingale avoided this pitfall by combining objective analysis as a statistician with an appeal to emotion. Rather than asking herself how she could get her feelings across to the audience, she asked what already made them feel the way she needed them to. Nightingale conveyed a sense of tragedy. She understood that this sense of tragedy already existed in her audience's mind, through shared knowledge of epidemics such as bubonic plague and events such as the sinking of the *Birkenhead*. Rather than try to conjure emotion from square one, she simply targeted preexisting pools of emotion, making a logical case that her audience should feel as bad or worse about the ongoing medical mismanagement in the army.

So, given her consistent, deliberate use of emotional numbers, what are we to think when she celebrates "dry statistics"? Perhaps it is the curse of knowledge. Nightingale has seen the positive effects of un-dry statistics but simply doesn't realize what she is doing to give them force. The expert home cook often writes lousy recipes when asked how to cook one of their crowd-pleasing dishes, not because they are trying to protect their family secrets, but because they can't imagine how many things a more naïve cook wouldn't think to do.

But when people advocate for "dry statistics" there seems to be a component of identity and ideology. There is a purity to the idea of "dry statistics" that numbers people swear by. Analytical people want to believe that their hard-earned numbers will carry the day. And historians have emphasized that in Victorian culture statistics were embraced with a moral fervor that occasionally became almost religious. Indeed the advantages of a more statistical society were clear. A simple example: Farr, Nightingale, and colleagues set up a common reporting structure for deaths in hospitals and the broader community that allowed people to say, for example, that heart disease is a bigger killer than cancer. Without the infrastructure they created, we wouldn't be able to answer questions about how many of our citizens die from heart attacks or colon cancer. These questions seem obvious now, but at the time they transformed what social activists could discuss and what government officials had to acknowledge.

Luckily Nightingale ignored the advice she gave to her friend Farr, and trailblazed a different kind of emotional argument. Aristotle divided persuasion tools into logos (cold logical argument) and pathos (appeals to emotion). Nightingale found a middle way by wrapping a cold, logical statistic inside a precise, numerically similar, heartrending analogy.

Aristotle's pathos and logos could not occupy the rhetorical stage at the same time; pathos and logos did not interact. Nightingale bridged the gap and managed to connect logos to an afterburner of pathos. She created sad numbers. Impolite numbers. Angry numbers. Tragic numbers.

We are no more likely to know what to *feel* about a number than we are to know what to think about a number. We used fathoms to understand how to think about abstract numbers; "Turkey is 785,000 square kilometers" doesn't help us understand the world as much as "Turkey is twice the size of California." In this section of the book we will give you some tools for helping people *feel* something about numbers. And feeling is important because in a world filled with things that need to be accomplished, our feelings about our alternatives lead us to which one we will choose and how fervently we will pursue it and respond to setbacks. The process of producing an emotional number starts by looking, as Nightingale did, for preexisting pools of emotion.

Comparatives, Superlatives, and Category Jumpers

Their new center is 7'8" tall.	Their new center is 2 inches taller than Yao Ming.

Portland, Oregon, spiked temperatures of 112 and 115 on successive days in June 2011.	Portland, Oregon, spiked temperatures of 112 and 115 on successive days in June 2011. That's almost like living in Death Valley, California, where the average July day has a high of 116.

Yao Ming is tall. Chevy Corvettes are fast. Death Valley is hot. Making a number emotional is easier than it might, at first, appear as long as we remember one simple principle: emotion comes from emotion. So all you have to do is find some comparison that already carries the emotion you need, and use your numbers to justify why the emotion ought to transfer. This doesn't just work in Florence Nightingale's domain of tragic deaths, which come freighted with emotion. We also have emotional associations with many objective qualities: "tall," "fast," "cold," "expensive," "important." Creating the right emotion simply requires us to pick the right comparatives.

Here's an example of how emotion guides our assessment of a seemingly mundane number—attendance figures at a national park.

Great Smoky Mountains National Park receives 12.5 million visitors in a typical year.	Great Smoky Mountains National Park is the most-visited national park in the U.S., with more than twice as many visitors as the Grand Canyon, which comes in second.

Great Smoky Mountains National Park receives 12.5 million visitors a year.

We don't feel much about the number in the left panel. "Okay, good for the Great Smokies" might be a typical reaction. We aren't predisposed to feeling much about the park—it doesn't have the ring of something like the Grand Canyon, which has a huge role in popular culture. It's a bucket-list destination; we've seen friends post pictures of it online.

But since Great Smoky does have the stats on its side, we can aim directly for the Grand Canyon comparison and all the emotion that comes with it. We might ho-hum through hearing about some number of millions—aren't there millions of people always visiting everywhere—but when we hear that it's twice as much as the Grand Canyon and 3 times as many as Yellowstone, it has our attention.

Once we're there, we might look into what makes the park so popular. It's big and accessible, with many entrances; it's along a major highway in a population-dense region; it's near a lot of other tourist attractions like Dollywood; and it's free to visit! That this combination puts it ahead of places that have much more iconic sights and features may help us rethink how to drive tourism. But it never gets our attention until we know it beats what we think of as "major parks."

Many of our favorite examples from the book employ these kinds of comparisons. We don't understand quite how a large ship such as the *Ever Given* could block the Suez Canal until we compare it to the Empire State Building—something we feel is massive, gargantuan, a real structure and a force to be reckoned with. We don't understand just how rare female CEOs are until we compare them with Jameses, just a random guy's name we'd expect to encounter only occasionally. African Americans live with stereotyping and discrimination, but many non-minority readers won't appreciate the full weight of that burden until we compare it with trying to be hired as a felon—something we feel carries a heavy weight. The comparison gets attention.

Superlatives, Incomparables

The need for bringing emotion to numbers is illustrated best by situations where the numbers are quite obvious yet the object described by the numbers is not getting sufficient respect. How do you motivate your audience in a situation where the numbers show you are best by a long shot and yet the crowd sees you as *perhaps a bit better*.

Sometimes #1s seem to get too much respect. Everest is indeed the tallest mountain in the world, but it probably gets too much emotional mileage from that. As we saw in the "two-story house" translation in the human-scale chapter, its lead over K2 is smallish. Many superlatives are like this. Barry Bonds had 7 more home runs than Hank Aaron, a lead that could be erased by a couple of inches in fence height.

More interesting from the standpoint of understanding emotion are situations where we are dealing with super-superlatives, which we call "incomparables." These incomparables are the biggest and the best . . . and second place is not even close. When we have such a figure, we should emphasize it—indeed it would seem hard to miss the opportunity.

But we miss it.

You probably learned in school that the Nile is the longest river in the world but that the Amazon is the largest by volume. That probably made you feel that the rivers are equally distinguished; that they just have different domains of superiority. But in reality the Nile barely, tenuously edges into the #1 spot as longest river. In length, the Nile is barely longer than the Amazon—in fact, by some measures, it's not even #1, while on any metric of size—"largest"/widest/highest water volume—the Amazon has no rival.

The Amazon is the world's largest river by a substantial margin. Four of the next 11 biggest rivers already flow into it. If the other 7—including the Congo, the Ganges, and the Yangtze—were combined into one super-river, the Amazon would still be bigger.

This analysis of the top 11 rivers eliminates any question of what river is the biggest or which one should make us feel the most awe. Note that we did this by adding up the erstwhile competitors and showing that the Amazon was yet bigger.

For another example of this principle in the realm of automobiles, consider Tesla, a company that investors believe has so much potential to revolutionize the industry that its market cap in 2021 was greater than that of its next few automotive competitors combined (including GM, Ford, Toyota, Honda, and VW). See how the translations above phrase these astonishing leads in concrete terms and left out the math? For a real super-superlative, we should be able to establish its dominance without any (visible) numbers at all.

Another strategy is to subtract some advantage and show that the incomparable is still in the lead "with one hand tied behind its back." For example, hockey player Wayne Gretzky, "the great one," scored the most goals in NHL history . . . and would remain the number-one scorer in NHL history even if you subtracted every single one of his solo goals from the record, because the number of points he scored from assists is even larger. He was a solo star who was an awesome team player.

But other times, dominating your present competition isn't enough. You need to compare your number to something else entirely.

Category Jumpers

In terms of economic prowess, California leads all the other 49 states in GDP.	If California were a free-standing country, it would be the 5th-largest economy in the world.

No matter how much bigger California's economy is than the next-best state, there's still a limit to how strong we can imagine a state economy can be. But when we think of California sitting, on its own, at the big countries' table at the economic summit, we get a sense of its true influence.

In comparing California to a country, we use a technique we call category jumping—comparing something to an entirely different class of competitors, in the case of California comparing a state to nations.

Back in his youth, Arnold Schwarzenegger, bodybuilder turned celebrity turned governor of the state Nation of California, once said of another bodybuilder who was a formidable competitor, "Those aren't arms, they're legs." Arms as big as legs, cities as big as nations, a sister as annoying as an entire elementary-school lunchroom. Category jumpers bring extra emotion and extra respect back to their interactions in their home category.

> In 2020, Apple was at one point valued at over $2 trillion. Imagine Apple as a country, with its shareholders as citizens and its citizens' sole source of wealth their Apple stock. The total wealth of Apple would still be ahead of 150/171 countries, including Norway, South Africa, Thailand, and Saudi Arabia.

If you ever had a doubt that corporations are major economic players who might be tricky for governments to handle, that single statistic about Apple is good to chew on.

Your goal is to find the largest category that your number can dominate, then let it. Suppose our goal is to get people to understand the impact of the greenhouse-gas emissions produced by livestock. We might consider other categories: Are they as big as a city? A region? A country? Small country or large? An ideal frame of reference combines accuracy and surprise.

Livestock are responsible for 14.5% of global greenhouse-gas emissions.	"If cows were a country," they would be the third-highest producer of greenhouse emissions among all nations. They produce more emissions than Saudi Arabia or Australia or India, "and surpass every country in the European Union combined. They lag behind only China and America." (Based on Steven Chu.)

The first stat looks unremarkable. We're used to seeing agriculture as an economic sector, and 14.5% makes it look like a minor factor among many.

But when *New Yorker* writer Tad Friend challenges us to imagine "if cows were a country," then suddenly addressing the cattle industry comes to feel unavoidable. We can't imagine a solution to climate change that doesn't involve reforming India, the EU, or major oil-producing countries like Saudi Arabia. After this category-jumping comparison, we won't be able to imagine a solution that doesn't involve reforming the "nation of cows" that looms larger than any of them.

With well-targeted category jumping, numbers people can take their skills to another realm. Numbers-minded people often distrust figurative language because it feels frivolous and airy, but the comparisons we looked at are defensible and firm. At its best, category jumping can combine different domains to yield new insights. If you can simultaneously follow your emotions and the numbers, you can bridge worlds.

Emotional Amplitude: Selecting Combos That Hit the Right Notes Together

This section so far has focused on finding the right emotional note— a single comparable with a known feeling attached to it. We know people feel "tall" from the Eiffel Tower, "tragic" from the *Titanic*, and "exhausted" from 6 hours straight of Zoom calls. Compare our quantity to these things, and we can evoke the same emotion.

But sometimes, rather than one emotional note, we want a whole symphony, we want elements working together to find a resonance that's deeper and fuller than any one element on its own.

Consider President Dwight Eisenhower's famous "Chance for Peace" speech, delivered to the American Society of Newspaper Editors on April 16, 1953:

> *Every gun that is made, every warship launched, every rocket fired signifies, in the final sense, a theft from those who hunger and are not fed, those who are cold and are not clothed.*
>
> *This world in arms is not spending money alone. It is spending the sweat of its laborers, the genius of its scientists, the hopes*

of its children. The cost of one modern heavy bomber is this: a modern brick school in more than 30 cities. It is 2 electric power plants, each serving a town of 60,000 population. It is 2 fine, fully equipped hospitals. It is some 50 miles of concrete highway.

We pay for a single fighter plane with a half-million bushels of wheat. We pay for a single destroyer with new homes that could have housed more than 8,000 people . . . This is not a way of life at all, in any true sense. Under the cloud of threatening war, it is humanity hanging from a cross of iron.

Eisenhower was already ahead of his time in making concrete conversions, showing the cost of war not in dollars but in real things that can transform lives. But his speech is more than a random collection of parts. By itself, a school, a power plant, a hospital, or a road is a budget item. Together, they start to look like a better society, a brighter way of life.

The key to these kinds of translations is choosing elements that are close enough in theme that they complement each other, but not so close that they're redundant. The Beatles wouldn't be the same if they were just four Lennons or four McCartneys—the combo worked because each instrument, each member of the ensemble, complemented the others.

Not every topic with a harmonious comparison is as grand as a revival of America's peacetime infrastructure. It can be as simple as sugar.

The dry statistic:	The translation:
A 12-oz. serving of Ocean Spray Cran-Apple juice has 44 grams of sugar, or 11 teaspoons.	Drinking a 12-oz. serving of Ocean Spray Cran-Apple juice is the sugar equivalent of 3 glazed donuts from Krispy Kreme . . . plus 4 sugar cubes.

If you only compare the juice to a few donuts, or to 19 sugar cubes, the impact wouldn't be nearly as powerful. 3 donuts is a lot, but not disgusting. 11 sugar cubes is a lot, but on their own, they're a little abstract—unless you're a horse, you probably don't consume sugar in that form.

But, working in harmony, the donuts and sugar build up to something that grabs our attention. Already, it's a little sweet for adult palates—we can imagine not feeling so healthy after eating 3 donuts. But then we keep crunching 4 cubes of sugar. The message of this sickly symphony is clear: despite the words "apple" and "juice," we are not dealing with a healthy beverage.

We could have also told you that Ocean Spray Cran-Apple juice and Coca-Cola have around the same amount of sugar, and while you might have been surprised by that fact, it wouldn't have told you much about *just* how much sugar drinking either one entails. And they don't have exactly the same amount of sugar. In a 12-ounce serving, the Cran-Apple juice has an extra teaspoon. Imagine a coworker patiently jiggering a coffee spoon into the tiny opening on a can of Coke to slide in an extra teaspoon of sugar.

Emotionally resonant combos also work for serious issues, as we learn from Nightingale and from the modern-day medical translation below, which highlights a life-saving intervention for a little-studied cause of death.

In the United States every year, nearly 270,000 patients die from sepsis. Kaiser Permanente in Northern California recently developed a protocol that reduces sepsis deaths by 55%! If it were rolled out to every hospital in the U.S. it would save 147,000 lives per year. That's more lives saved than saving each year every woman with breast cancer and every man with prostate cancer . . . combined!

Either prostate cancer or breast cancer would feel weighty already, but in combination we get the feeling "this affects you" no matter our reader's gender. The two cancers parallel each other: Breast cancer is the #2 cancer cause of death for women in the United States, and prostate cancer the #2 for men. They have similar profiles in our mental pictures—both cancers have marches, donation drives, awareness months, and ribbon campaigns.

What if we could save *everyone* who died of *both* these diseases? We can imagine how wonderful the cure would be. Once we see that we already have discovered a medical intervention that saves that many people (and many, many more), there's only one possible reaction: "do this immediately!"

At a certain point adding notes to a chord starts to feel inharmonious as in the following example. Suppose you are an entrepreneur who has a product that is useful to residents of cities with populations over 5 million each, and that you are trying to emphasize to your team that your company needs to look to China.

The population of China's largest cities is as big as the population of Tokyo, Delhi, Seoul, Manila, Mumbai, São Paulo, Mexico City, Cairo, and Los Angeles—combined.

This is more cacophony than symphony. By the time we get to Manila, we're already struggling to get these elements in tune with each other. Each additional city is a very different place—each a long flight across water—and we have no way to do the mental mash-up. "What do Tokyo, Delhi, Seoul, Manila, Mumbai, São Paulo, Mexico City, Cairo, and Los Angeles have in common?" seems like one of those aggravating riddles that actually doesn't have an answer.

Consider this simpler example:

In western Europe, there are only 4 cities worth pursuing: London, Paris, Madrid, and Barcelona. China has 17 cities larger than Barcelona, and 6 of them are larger than London or Paris.

This translation asks us to consider just 4 European cities, and they're all part of a set—they've been in communication with each other for centuries, they're part of our cultural tour of Europe. And, as with any great comparison, they also point at something wrong with our way of thinking. How many books and movies have featured the great cities of western Europe? How much do we know about them, even if we haven't visited?

But few of us can even name all the Londons or Parises of China, let alone its Barcelonas.* Any person or organization with a global focus will understand they have a lot of catching up to do to understand that world.

---

* Try it. Which ones do you even recognize?: Harbin, Suzhou, Shenyang, Foshan, Hangzhou, and Dongguan are all 20–40% bigger than Barcelona, but most Americans don't recognize any of them. (This would be like a European not recognizing the American cities Philadelphia, Miami, or Dallas.) The six cities bigger than London or Paris are: Shanghai, Beijing, Chongqing, Tianjin, Guangzhou, and Shenzhen. (Not recognizing these cities is like a non-American not recognizing New York City or Los Angeles.)

Make It Personal: "This Is About You"

Our brains are complex webs of associations, and we can access a piece of info in many different ways. The more a new fact connects with the existing network of associations in our brains, the more likely we are to remember it. We might forget an anecdote about a stranger because it makes few connections with our existing associations, but we won't forget a piece of gossip about our cousin.

There's one complex network that is larger and quicker to access than all others—the self. We've been thinking about ourselves our whole lives. (In fact, there were entire years during junior high when we weren't capable of thinking about much else.) So if a new piece of info has something to do with *us*, it will be more easily and thoroughly processed. It hits even closer to home than our actual home—we can take a vacation away from our home, but not from our*selves*.

The most effective communicators find ways to make the abstract personal. Consider the warning that law schools give to motivate first-year law students concerning the rigors of their program. Hearing that "the first-year dropout rate is 33%" is an abstract statistic. "Look to your left, look to your right. One of the three of you won't be joining us next fall" wakes up the self. We feel something.

There's a 20% chance of experiencing a mental illness in a given year, and a 50% chance of being diagnosed with a mental illness in your lifetime.	To a group sitting at a conference table: Say, "For every 5 people, 1 of you will be diagnosed with a mental illness this year. At some point in your lifetime, either you or the person across from you will be diagnosed with a mental illness."

Suppose the numbers have nothing to do with me. Even if the numbers are not *my* numbers, the right pitch might conceivably tempt me to think about how your numbers would affect my life. It's intriguing to imagine alternate versions of ourselves.

In the next example, someone—let's say a development economist—wants us to understand the precarious position of a Kenyan family. That may be as simple as asking listeners to imagine spending the majority of their money on things like food.

Average earnings in Kenya are about $7,000 per year (compared with $68,000 in the United States). Kenyans spend about 50% of their income on food.	If you spent the same portion of your weekly income on food as Kenyans do, 7 days of eating would cost you $650 for dishes like cornmeal porridge and potato pea mash. How easily could you pay your other bills if food sucked up that much of your resources?

As households grow wealthier, they end up spending proportionately less on necessities such as food and shelter, and proportionately more on things like education and transportation.

People are willing in most circumstances to join you in a mental journey. In the unfolding story below, the fact that I am imagining myself acting adds drama and keeps attention focused on the story.

Jeff Bezos is worth $198 billion.

Let's imagine if each step of a staircase represents $100,000 in the bank. Most people, including 1 in 2 Americans and 89% of the world, can't even step onto the first step of the staircase because they have less. After 4 steps, we've lost over 75% of Americans. Fewer than 1 in 10 people will ever reach the 10th step: a million dollars.

Now put on your most comfortable hiking shoes. You'd have to climb for almost 3 hours before reaching the net worth of a billionaire.

After spending 9 hours a day climbing steps for 2 months, you'd have Ironman-level quads as you finally reach the wealth of Jeff Bezos.

The visual of your Ironman quads might make you tell the Jeff Bezos story to a friend who would otherwise never have known about his wealth.

Unfolding stories are even better when people are mentally living out their own story, complete with stages—video game–level accomplishment and rewards.

If you, like the typical American, drive about 40 miles per day in a car with typical fuel efficiency, then replacing your car with a Prius will save you 50% in gas.	If you, like the typical American, drive 40 miles per day or more, in a car with typical gas efficiency, then replacing your car with a Prius would mean that a month from now, you'll have saved enough to take someone out to a fancy dinner. In 6 months, you can go on a weekend getaway or buy yourself a smartwatch. In a year, you'll have saved enough to pay for your annual gym membership.

If a piece of information naturally relates to the people you are presenting it to, don't neglect to highlight that connection. If it's not about them, many times they can be persuaded to play along at home—to imagine themselves in someone else's story. All data is more engaging if people can use it to imagine themselves taking action and reaping the benefits (or paying the costs) of their actions.

Turn Your Statistic Into a Verb:
Layer Actions on Top of Concrete Nouns

While "distance to the moon" or "3,871 flights of stairs" may seem concrete, our senses and memories don't give us a true sense of how far that actually is. They're abstract numbers. To make sure a large object counts as "concrete," express it in actions we know. "Verbing it" is about making sure that objects and actions are made concrete by ensuring that our audience mentally "sees" them in motion.

Bring Your Number into the Room with a Demonstration

Things we experience lodge in our memories more deeply and more easily than things we are told. Moreover, they *become stories*, things we can remember and repeat. What happened at the meeting today? "We walked back and forth with lengths of copper wire for five minutes" is an anecdote you tell your friends or family when they ask how your classes were. "We saw a bar graph" isn't.

Activate the Senses

The current operating system for programming industrial robots is from 1969. You want to convince people that that is ludicrously out of date . . .	As people enter the meeting room, play music from 1969. During your discussion section, say: "We call those 'classic' rock and roll songs. Do you want your tech to be classic?"	To the music soundtrack, add visuals: Show ads for cars from 1969, clock radios, a computer, rotary-dial telephones, television sets with big dials. Serve them a TV dinner with Baked Alaska for dessert. Remind them: "If you miss an episode of a TV show, you may never see it again."

When we say "play music from 1969," by the way, we mean a full spectrum, from good to bad. Some of the music was forgettable—the #1 song was *Sugar, Sugar* by a group called the Archies that didn't really exist. They were cartoon characters, and you could see their show at 8:00 a.m., if you woke up in time. If you missed it, you missed it—no streaming, no YouTube, not even TiVo or a VCR.

But it also had some classics. *Get Back*, by the Beatles; *Honky Tonk Women*, by the Rolling Stones; *Hooked on a Feeling*, by B. J. Thomas. You even had a Michael Jackson single (the Jackson 5 classic *I Want You Back*), but he was just an 11-year-old fronting his family band, and Neil Armstrong was the only person making a moon walk famous.

It was truly a different era—but with the exact same software running the majority of robots in the world. Playing the music from the era would make the audience feel "old" in a way that reading a number wouldn't, triggering memories, nostalgia, or, in younger audiences, just a sense of "oh yeah, that kind of music Grandma likes."

If you had more time and really wanted to make the point stick, you could go with the all-senses demonstration in the rightmost column—bringing the look, sound, feel, and even tastes of the era into play. It would be hard to sit in that immersive demonstration and think, Yeah, the technology from this era is probably fine.

Make Your Audience Experience the Statistic

People can easily forget what they're told. They have a better chance of remembering what they see. But something they *do* becomes part of their experience in a much deeper way, getting embedded in their memory and instincts.

To demonstrate how tragic it is to waste a microsecond, Grace Hopper cut a wire the length that a signal could travel in that time to show to her programmers. A microsecond goes by so fast we can't even register it. But 984 feet of copper wire can't escape our notice. Especially in the early days of computing, when resources were precious, this helped programmers be conscious of waste that they couldn't notice directly.

Hopper's 984 feet of wire is *showing* the number. But if she wanted to make it into an even more memorable demonstration, she could have taken it a step further and really made her programmers experience the number. For example, if she'd tied teams of two programmers together and made them race this distance in a three-legged race. Even the fittest navy midshipman (Hopper was a rear admiral as well as a programmer) would have trouble getting through 984 feet of a three-legged race in good shape. Afterward she could tell them, "The distance you raced is what an electrical signal travels in a microsecond. Don't waste those!"

Or if she were teaching a less athletic class, she could select two students to stand at opposite ends of the classroom and assign a third student to walk between them, spooling the thread around them as the class continued. It would take around five minutes— long enough for the point to sink in.

From "a microsecond," to a concrete piece of wire, to actually having to travel that length of wire, each level of translation makes the statistic easier to understand and harder to ignore.

The next example deals with fractions of seconds, an amount of time we can observe but can't fully appreciate until we change them into an experience:

A batter has roughly a quarter of a second—250 milliseconds—to decide whether to swing at a pitch, and even less time (150 milliseconds) to take the swing.

Clap your hands as quickly as you can for just one second. Most people can clap 4 or 5 times. Suppose you can clap 4 times a second. A major league batter has only 1 of those claps to decide whether to swing at a pitch. By the time you've clapped twice, the play is over.

Extra credit: *to help someone understand this speed, designate that person as the batter, and choose another person as the pitcher. Give the pitcher a few moments to practice clapping 4 times per second. Have the batter stand up, close their eyes, and pretend to hold a baseball bat. When ready, ask the pitcher to say, "I'm winding up," pause briefly, and clap twice. The play is over.*

(At this point, the batter says, "That's ridiculous," and proceeds to throw the imaginary bat on the ground.)

Keep in mind that demos are best used for key points—the things you want people to remember as *the main point or the epiphany* of a meeting. A friend remembered an example like this from his Little League days, when his coach was trying to prepare him to face a precocious pitcher who threw 70+ mph in sixth grade. (Most sixth graders are mastering the 50 mph fastball, so encountering a 70+ mph fastball was like suddenly being promoted to the high-school team without having had a high-school growth spurt.)

The gist of the lesson was "This is how fast you have to react, plus you have to physically swing the bat. You should prepare to react very quickly, and even then, there's not much chance you'll hit the ball. If you haven't started swinging by the first clap, don't. Either way, it will probably feel bad and that's okay. You're not messing up; you're just limited by physics."

Here's another example from the realm of athletics, which shows the blink-of-an-eye margins that distinguish Olympic runners.

In the 2016 Olympics in Rio de Janeiro, Usain Bolt won the 200-meter dash with a time of 19.78. The silver medalist crossed .24 seconds after Bolt and runners 3–7 followed in the next .21 seconds. The final runner crossed at 20.43.

Clap your hands as quickly as you can for just 1 second. Most people can clap 4 times a second. This is how to think of the ending of the race:
Clap 1—Bolt wins the race.
Clap 2—the silver medalist crosses, but so do the bronze medalist and the next 4 runners.
Clap 3—the eighth-fastest person in the world at 200 meters crosses, hopelessly out of contention, and the race is over.

The translation in the following box is based on a demonstration created by a friend of Chip's who, at the time, was a sophomore in college. That year the National Endowment of the Arts was in hot water because it had supported an artist who was creating art that many regarded as anti-religious. The friend was an engineer, not a political science major, but he demonstrates a more sophisticated understanding of federal budgets and expenses than the vast majority of professional political pundits.

In 2016, $148 million was allocated to the National Endowment for the Arts. This accounted for .004% of the federal budget, which was $3.9 trillion in total.	Said to someone who is complaining about the egregious misallocation of citizens' tax dollars to fund offensive art: "Someone earning $60,000 a year pays about $6,300 in federal income taxes. The 25 cents I am handing you now is your annual contribution to the NEA. I'm personally refunding your money because I'm tired of hearing you rant."

The person receiving the quarter doesn't even realize they're taking part in a demonstration until it's too late. They might earnestly believe that the NEA budget is a problem, but it's very hard for them to have the same belief about a quarter, which isn't even tipping money. The next time they give a dollar to a street musician, they might think quadrupling the NEA budget would be just fine.

Make It Personal—Pick People in the Room

Behavioral science shows that we pay much more attention when things are close by and specific. If a statistic applies to a percentage or fraction of people, it doesn't instinctively feel real, let alone consequential. But something that's happening to us, or the people with us, feels as real as it gets. That's why law professors say "one of you will not make it to graduation," instead of just citing matriculation rates. If you want an audience invested in a problem, you can use substitution and role-playing to get them to put skin in the game.

In New Jersey, high-school teacher Nicholas Ferroni devised a lesson to help his male students understand the impact of a gender imbalance in Congress.

The U.S. Congress is 73% male and frequently passes legislation that affects the lives of women.	If you have a large group, select a subgroup of 3 women and 1 man. Have them vote on issues that only affect the men in the group.

Just the simple reversal is likely to make the men feel squeamish—and introduce them to the status quo and the reality of the women.

Here's a demonstration that goes in the opposite direction, making us imagine being on the high end of a power dynamic.

Amazon founder Jeff Bezos increased his fortune by $75 billion in 2020.	Think about $25,000: how many weeks do you have to work to make that much? How dramatically would your life change if someone gave you $25,000? Would you finally be debt-free? If you had to give away $25,000, how many people's lives could you save by paying for their food, rent, or medical bills? That's what Jeff Bezos made in the time it took you to read this (11 seconds).

This demonstration takes a while to sink in, but it's powerful when it does—in the time you can imagine having transformative amounts of money, a billionaire actually gains that much. The more time you sit contemplating the question, the more he racks up.

This experience is bound to make a lot of people angry that so much money is flowing to one person. Others might think he deserves to enjoy the benefits of what he has created. But no matter how we feel, this tells us that we can't think of the wealthiest people in the world in terms of our everyday conception of "rich"— they're dealing with an entirely different level of money than our instincts are used to.

Show Things You Can't Put Into Words

Sometimes a demonstration can translate sets of numbers so complex they could never fit in a slide deck. One of our favorite stories came from Jon Stegner, who found an ingenious way to demonstrate how the procurement system at his company was overspending on a huge swath of products.

"We're wasting millions, perhaps 10s of millions on an inefficient procurement system. Here's a 9-tabbed spreadsheet that summarizes my findings."	"Come see my collection of the 424 different gloves that our company is currently ordering. This represents just one minor product that we purchase . . ."

First, he assigned a summer intern to look at one simple item among the countless categories of things the company purchased: gloves. The gloves were used during specific operations on the assembly line to protect workers against sharp and hot objects. Across all its factories, it turned out the company purchased 424 different types of gloves, and often paid wildly different prices for similar gloves from different suppliers. Putting all these data points into one Excel document would be a chore. Putting it into a text or speech would be impossible.

But Stegner found a very simple way to express both the complex data and the simple message. He sent the intern to go track down one of each glove, attached price tags to them, and poured the gloves out onto a conference room table and invited the leaders, one by one, to come see the "Glove Shrine." Anyone could see at a quick glance or upon deeper examination that the procurement system for gloves seriously needed to be revamped. It was easy to see a black pair for $3.22 and next to it an identical-looking pair with a $10.55 price tag. Because the Glove Shrine was a physical demonstration of what was actually happening, the point made was undeniable.

The minute anyone saw the Glove Shrine, they immediately jumped to a question, the very one Stegner had wanted them to ask: "If we're wasting this much money on gloves, what else are we wasting money on?"

The demonstration ended up going out on a "campaign tour" through the company—to executive offices and factory floors. Soon all the decision makers understood that they needed to overhaul the purchasing process—all without Stegner having to fight tooth and nail to convince them. You can't argue with a Glove Shrine.

And that's the point of demos, really. "Dry" statistics don't help people to see something a different way ("You mean we're really buying all these kinds of gloves?!"), and they can't move people to care ("Well, what else are we wasting money on?").

In acting out numbers, by seeing and touching their concrete manifestations, people are able to understand them at a visceral level—how long 984 feet is, how scary it is to face a 75 mph fastball, how redundant 424 kinds of gloves can be, how *looooong* ago 1969 was (apologies to those who personally *remember* 1969). If we want to move people with our numbers, we can bring the numbers into the room for an up-close and personal encounter.

Avoid Numbing by Converting Your Number to a Process That Unfolds Over Time

From 1999 to 2001, venture capitalists in Silicon Valley raised $204 billion, more than 4 times as many investment dollars as they had previously. Would they go on to match the industry's average annual returns of 18%, turning that investment into $1.3 trillion by 2012? That's a massive number, yet considering VCs had helped create powerhouses like Intel, and Apple, Cisco, and Netscape, it wasn't immediately obvious whether that outcome was likely or unlikely.

And then, a writer at *Fortune* turned it into a process.

> Are historical rates of return from VC investments likely to hold given the amount of money that is chasing deals? $204 billion of investment would require an eventual payoff of $1.3 trillion by 2012.

> "Think about it this way. eBay is one of the few successes to emerge from the dot-com boom. At its peak, eBay had a $16 billion market value, and its venture backer, Benchmark Capital, made more than $4 billion on its investment. So how many eBays would have to be taken public by the end of the decade for venture investors to achieve 18% returns? More than 325. *That's roughly one eBay every 10 days between now and 2012.*"

The updated version of this is launching 3 Facebooks a month, for 8 years in a row. The takeaway of both versions? *Not gonna happen.* This translation spreads out the answer into recognizable servings, each offering a full punch.

As numbers get higher, each increase sparks less awe, a phenomenon known as *psychological numbing.* Psychologist Paul Slovic has studied how our compassion for victims of tragedies diminishes as the numbers go up, partly due to an inability to attach meaning to large numbers in the way we can to just 1 of a thing. Earning your first $1 million is a triumph, but your 6th million is less triumphant. Your 57th million might go unnoticed. To convey a large number while still inspiring awe at its size, consider converting to an unfolding process. Make every million feel like your first.

Revisiting Firearms: Show How a Process Might Unfold

There are more than 400 million firearms in the U.S. That's enough for every man, woman, and child to own one, with 70 million remaining.	There are more than 400 million firearms in the U.S. That's enough for every man, woman, and child to own one, with enough left over that you could give one to every baby born in America for the next 20 years.

We already translated the first part of the stat—distributing one firearm to every man, woman, and child—which takes us to 330 million. But converting to a process helps bring home the actual scale of the 70 million surplus.

Express Your Number as the Cumulative Outcome of Common Actions

Our everyday routines, habits, and processes are familiar to us, making them perfect building blocks for imagining things we haven't directly experienced.

It's an old trick: anthropologists looking at words that different cultures had developed for distance noted that many involved a process. For example, the Nicobarese, who live on a chain of islands in the Indian Ocean, use "the distance covered while drinking a young coconut." Another culture measured distance by the time it took to chew a betel nut (Karen of Southeast Asia). One northern Scandinavian culture, the Saami of Lapland, had a particularly elegant set of metrics: journeys of a few days were described in "human days," but if the distances grew vast, they might be described in larger units, "reindeer days" (the distance reindeer could travel in a day), or "wolf-days" (the largest unit of all). But the most familiar metric, and the word most sorely needed in English, is one they used to measure partial-day journeys: they gauged them based on the number of stops required for coffee.

Travel estimates built on everyday processes are useful because everyone can imagine the process and get a sense of distance without having to calculate and convert.

In our complex modern world, we can still use the same trick—expressing numbers as the process of simple actions that evoke: the muscle memory of a well-rehearsed routine.

From Charles Fishman: Buying a bottle of Evian is 3,970 times more expensive than filling the bottle from your faucet.	"In San Francisco, the municipal water comes from inside Yosemite National Park. It's so good the EPA doesn't require San Francisco to filter it. If you bought and drank a bottle of Evian, you could refill that bottle once a day for 10 years, 5 months, and 21 days with San Francisco tap water before that water would cost $1.35."

This simple conversion changes a multiplier that is way too large to grasp into a process that's impossible to forget.

Six Sigma is 3.4 defects per million objects.	To achieve Six Sigma as a baker, imagine baking a batch of 2 dozen chocolate chip cookies every night. You could do that for 37 years before finding a cookie that is burned, raw, or doesn't have the perfect number of chips.

We don't have an intuitive sense of a million objects, but the baking conversion shows a layperson just how exacting Six Sigma is. This could easily be adjusted with different processes and multipliers to match different audiences. For a Major League Baseball pitcher, it would be going 98 years without a single pitch outside the strike zone (and without giving up a single hit . . . 20+ gems a season).

Group the Steps of Your Process So That You Can Feel the Weight

Imagine loading 100 apples into a large bucket. Each one feels like almost nothing—a third of a pound, smaller than the smallest weight you can find at a gym. But pick up the bucket at the end, and it feels heavy.

Then, keep loading additional buckets onto a wooden pallet. At a certain point, you can't lift it anymore. It's now a job for a machine. 400 pounds might as well be 4,000 pounds, because neither is a weight you can do anything with.

For statistics that we want our audience to feel, we need to stay in bucket range—where they feel heavy, but not impossibly heavy.

1 murder occurs every 30 minutes in the United States.	Every day, 50 people are murdered.

Every 30 seconds, someone on social media posts a sad statistic that begins something like, "Every 30 seconds, This Bad Thing happens." It's not a bad instinct, the attempt to invoke the power-of-1 technique we highlighted in chapter 3. But one death in the abstract doesn't always carry much weight, especially with this format that is used so often it feels trite and gets tuned out.

Taking stock of the murder rate at the end of the day gets us to notice it again. 50 a day is a noteworthy number; it's big enough that it can't slip by us, but not big enough that we need our calculator.

It's possible to do both, showing both the accumulation and the individual instance. The *New York Times* did a particularly moving version of this to mark the date when the COVID-19 death toll hit 100,000. They devoted the entire front page to a huge, sprawling list of 1,000 names of people who died from COVID-19, covering six 20-inch columns, above and below the fold, taking up the full spread of the paper. The names were accompanied by short biographical details, as in this excerpt:

---

1 person dies from COVID every minute in the United States.

Robert Garff, 77, Utah, former speaker of the Utah House, auto executive and philanthropist • **Philip Thomas**, 48, Chicago, his Walmart co-workers were like family • **Alan Merrill**, 69, New York City, songwriter of "I Love Rock' n' Roll" • **Peter Sakas**, 67, Northbrook, Ill., ran an animal hospital • **Joseph Yaggi**, 65, Indiana, mentor and friend to many • **Mary Roman**, 84, Norwalk, Conn., shot-put champion and fixture in local politics • **Lorena Borjas**, 59, New York City, transgender immigrant activist • **James T. Goodrich**, 73, New York City, surgeon who separated conjoined twins • **Janice Preschel**, 60, Teaneck, N.J., founded a food pantry • **Jean-Claude Henrion**, 72, Atlantis, Fla., always rode Harley-Davidsons.

Rather than making the reader *imagine* a drip, drip, of one abstract victim every minute, the paper kept the reader engaged by citing something concrete and emotionally touching that made each person real and distinct, a bright light, the kind of person we'd be excited to share a drink with in a bar—before we remember that they'd been lost.

For the full effect, you would need to see the page in print: At the same time we are reading about individuals, line by line, our eyes see a huge page filled with these names and stories. It stretches as far as the eye can see—and as the *Times* notes, it takes 2 other spreads of similar size inside the section to list just 1,000 names out of the 100,000.

The individuals in the feature have weight. So, too, does the accumulation. Not every problem is as big as the COVID-19 crisis. The *New York Times* did not conjure the weight out of thin air, but they found a way to convey it so that any reader can feel it. This should be our aim when we have a weighty statistic that can be parceled out for full effect.

Offer an Encore

Have you ever been to a truly amazing rock concert? The band arranges a great set list that hits every angle of their work—just enough of the classics mixed with the newer hits, the centerpieces and the hidden diamonds, so the audience feels completely fulfilled, sure they've gotten more than their money's worth.

But then there's an encore. Sometimes it's a cover, sometimes it's a classic, but it gets the crowd to their feet. And they go home ecstatic because, after already being wowed to the fullest of their expectations, they still got something more.

When we really want to leave our audience impressed with a number, we can do something similar. The emotion isn't always ecstasy, and the mode isn't quite as entertaining, but the same method still works. We get numb to large quantities rather quickly if the news is delivered all at once. But if we can make a strong impression with less than our full figure, and deliver the reserve as an encore, both have a chance to sink in.

If everyone in the world ate as much meat as Americans, the amount of land required to raise livestock would equal 138% of the inhabitable land on Earth.	If everyone in the world ate as much meat as Americans, all inhabitable land on Earth would have to be used to raise livestock—and we'd still need more, an additional landmass as big as Africa and Australia combined.

We process the 138% all at once, as an overload. But if we imagine all inhabitable land on Earth used for grazing livestock—every field, forest, or neighborhood converted to a cattle farm—we intuitively know it's unsustainable. When we learn how even that is still an Africa and an Australia short of sustainable, the point sinks in even deeper.

We'd better learn to cook lentils.

The encore method is also perfect for making sense of large numbers, the kind we tend to blur instinctively. "It's like winning the lottery" has become such a cliché for long odds at this point we lose track of just how long the odds are. Here's a way to put things back into perspective:

Odds of winning Powerball: 1 in 292,201,338	Imagine having to guess which date someone is thinking of—any date between January 1 in the year 0001 (1 A.D.) and September 18 in the year 2667. If you match, you win the lottery prize. Just as they are about to hand you your check, they reveal that the fine print on your ticket requires passing one more hurdle. There are 300 identical envelopes on the wall. If you don't pick the one that holds your check, you receive nothing.

We could make the first task harder, but the pick-a-day scenario above is already hard enough. There's something particularly deflating about overcoming seemingly insurmountable odds and still finding you have almost no chance.

Encores work great in combination with other methods, including demonstrations and power-of-1 examples. If something already feels concrete and shocking, the encore hits even harder.

Like any other method, encores can be used for fun stats as well as serious ones. Here's something we love to imagine.

A frog can leap several times its own body size.	If you could leap like a frog, you would be able to dunk the ball from the 3-point line! . . . actually, from the 3-point line around your opponent's basket.

No NBA player in history—not Jordan, not LeBron, not even Air Bud—has dunked from the 3-point line. A free-throw dunk, much shorter, has only been accomplished a handful of times.

So already, this frog is leaps and bounds ahead of the competition. When we find that it's dunking from the 3-point line *at the other end of the court*, far beyond the frame of the camera, we're rising for a standing ovation.

Make People Pay Attention by Crystallizing a Pattern, Then Breaking It

When life doesn't match our predictions, we experience the most marvelous attention-grabbing treatment on Earth: surprise. Offering a surprising number will make it count. But as we've seen, audiences have diverse backgrounds and expectations. To break a rule as cleanly as a karate master breaks a board, first you've got to *set it up*.

We will call this technique "crystallize-break"—you have to first crystallize an idea in someone's mind before you can surprise them by breaking the expectation. We don't see the hero fight the bad guy until the bad guy has won a few matches. We aren't impressed with the third little pig's brick house until the first two get their houses blown down.

Steve Jobs had a flair for these techniques in the tech realm. Introducing the MacBook Air, he started out being unusually charitable toward its competition, the Sony TZ series. "They're good notebooks, and they're thin," he said.

He told the crowd that Apple had looked at all of the thinnest computers on the market. And he presented a table of their findings. The thin notebooks were adequately light, at about 3 pounds, but they had small screens and keyboards and slow processors, all things Apple wanted to fix with the Air.

Then he trotted out the graphics. A diagram appeared with a side view of the TZ. The thickest part was labeled 1.2 inches, and the machine tapered down to .8 inches in the front.

After he had crystallized in his audience's mind what "thin" looked like for the existing competitors, he broke the pattern with a graphic of the MacBook Air's dimensions. "This is the MacBook Air," he said, and the image below appeared.

The MacBook Air profile made the TZ series look positively hulking.

The crowd oohed and aahed and applause broke out. Jobs read off the dimensions: "0.76 inches in the back down to an unprecedented 0.16 inches in the front . . ."

And then he went in for the punch line. "And I want to point something out to you. The thickest part of the MacBook Air is still thinner than the thinnest part of the TZ."

Notice the beautiful application of the encore technique from the prior chapter. (And you know, given Jobs's perfectionism, that Apple must have burned out 3 mechanical engineers and 2 designers just to shave .04 inches off the height so Jobs could deliver his punch line: "our thickest is thinner than their thinnest!")

The powerful punch line in this presentation was only possible because the competition was built up first. Once we know what we're comparing to—the best side of the best device in the business—we can really understand the record-breaking nature of the MacBook Air. Without the "crystallize" before the "break," no one would have cared about the difference between .80 and .76.

"The dimensions of the TZ range from 1.2 inches to .8 inches; we beat that on average by half an inch."	"The thickest part of the MacBook Air is still thinner than the *thinnest* part of the TZ."

The brilliance of the technique is that it works for knowledgeable audiences as well as newbies. Jobs was presenting to techies, who could already appreciate the innovation, and to a broader public that might not have as much context.

If you had a sense of the general state of play in the tech industry, a complete survey of the competition would be relevant, even if the information wasn't new. It sets the scene, as well as answering questions you might already have: "Wait, how big is the Sony? What about the Lenovo? The Dell?" But if you didn't know already, you know by the time you need to. A great crystallization consolidates your audience—those familiar appreciate the precision, and the others appreciate the insight.

The following news story covers an artist, Romeo Santos, who is unknown to most U.S. readers but is so insanely popular with

Spanish-speaking audiences that he sold out two back-to-back shows at Yankee Stadium, at 50,000 tickets a night. No matter how much you know about music, this lede, from Larry Rohter of the *New York Times*, will help you figure out what 2 × 50,000 means:

> *Pink Floyd's* The Wall *couldn't do it, Jay Z got help from Justin Timberlake and Eminem, and Metallica didn't try. Selling out consecutive shows at Yankee Stadium, with its capacity of roughly 50,000, is nearly impossible for any pop music artist not named Paul McCartney. But Romeo Santos, who will perform there Friday and Saturday nights, is about to achieve that feat.*

A casual music listener will recognize at least some of these references, and know that they're big names. A musically knowledgeable person will be able to gain an even clearer picture of how high a bar back-to-back Yankee Stadium sellouts are. Both can experience the surprise of learning that an artist most *Times* readers haven't heard of is doing it. They will move their expectations about just how big Spanish-language music stars are—and pay more attention.

One reason Rohter's lede is so strong is that he knew what expectations fans might have, and hit pattern-setting examples that would reach Boomers, Gen Xers, and Millennials alike.

Many things come with a built-in set of cultural expectations. If we think of a "picnic," we likely imagine a red-and-white checked blanket, a wicker basket, sandwiches, and watermelon. Say "surfer" and our audience probably imagines a young White guy with long blond hair who says "dude" and is unlikely to be studying history. Give the audience a chance for that culturally expected mental image to crystallize and get fully activated, and they'll be more than surprised when you show them a break from those expectations—for example, an 83-year-old grandmother from Mali catching a wave.

But a skilled pattern maker can create an example even when we have no preexisting expectations, as Fareed Zakaria does below.

How do people in the world feel about free trade, and how does the typical American view differ? As you read below, trace how your expectations crystallize—and then change.

59% of Americans said that growing trade ties between countries are "very good" or "somewhat good."	Zakaria, citing a Pew survey: "Thumping majorities everywhere said that growing trade ties between countries are 'very good' or 'somewhat good'—91% in China, 85% in Germany, 88% in Bulgaria, 87% in South Africa, 93% in Kenya and so on. Of the 47 countries surveyed, the one that came in dead last was . . . America, at 59%. "The only country within 10 points of us was Egypt."

America is traditionally thought of as a pro-trade country, so seeing this pattern of percentages in the high 80s to low 90s might lead us to assume that the U.S. is in that range, or higher. Even if we're expecting a surprise, and think he's going to reveal that the United States is lower, we might start anticipating something in the mid-70s. Then he says "dead last," "59%," and "only country within 10 points." Surely these numbers fall below even our new expectations.

Now, what if he'd led with 59%? That wouldn't surprise us. Without points of comparison, it seems like a pro-trade majority. But presented in this way, it reveals something unexpected and highlights a surprising issue worth exploring.

Other problems that implicitly play with our expectations can be restructured to create more of a surprise.

What names are most common among Fortune 500 CEOs? John, James, and then . . . all women's names combined.

If we're not already talking about gender inequality, this could launch the discussion in an unexpected way. We're thinking about arbitrary facts, maybe even going through some lists of CEOs. Will it be Bill? Dave? Mike? Steve? When the punch line is revealed, it shows us what's been left out of the conversation, and points at something very wrong.

Here's another example we like—one that shows how little we know about our own body.

Nerve impulses travel through our body to our brain at the rate of 270 miles per hour. We typically take pride in the speed of our nervous systems.	"If a globe-spanning giant with its head in Baltimore and his toe off the South African coast were bitten on the foot by a shark on Monday, he would not feel the bite until Wednesday and would not react until Friday." (David Linden, Johns Hopkins)

We tend to think of nerve reactions as instantaneous, but in reality, they're much slower than an airplane. If we saw the shark bite the giant off the coast of Cape Town, we'd have time to change out of our swim clothes, catch a taxi, fly direct to Baltimore international airport, enjoy some crab cakes and beer in downtown Baltimore, and still whisper the bad news in the giant's ear before it felt the pain of the bite.

If you're like us, this assumption-shattering demonstration gave you a better understanding of your own body, and it should also change the way we look at movie monsters. The slow, lumbering Godzillas and King Kongs of the past are more realistic than the agile modern CGI versions.

Whatever the quantity you're trying to highlight—from laptop size to nerve speed—it stands out more when contrasted against the unspoken assumptions your audience brings to the scenario. Whenever possible, crystallize these assumptions right before the reveal. What does your audience think they know? How much money do they think they spend on the NEA? What entertainment industries do they think are the biggest? As soon as they get comfortable, you have the chance to break their expectations and create surprise.

And surprise is a powerful thing. If you've ever complained about "getting people's attention," whether the people are children in a classroom, voters in an election year, or frontline workers in a factory, surprise is just what you need. It's the emotion that gets you a whole lot of attention, all at once. Our eyes get wide. Our bodies freeze. You'll see mouths gaping, people dumbfounded, paralyzed. Surprise is a powerful thing. If it were a kind of torture, it would be illegal under the Geneva Convention. As it is, it's a powerful tool for influencing people to pay attention to the right things.

BUILD A SCALE MODEL

Map the Landscape by Finding the Landmarks

When you visit an unfamiliar city—London, Lisbon, Washington, DC—you generally encounter some form of a subway map. These maps are simple, brightly colored, and geographically inaccurate. You might learn to navigate a subway system and still have no idea how the city is really laid out. But that's a good sign—the map is telling you only what you need to know, how to get from Point A to Point B, without having to learn the whole landscape first. Over time, you can become a true local, explaining directions to clueless tourists, but in the meantime, you won't get lost on the way to your hotel.

When we're trying to orient people to an unfamiliar statistic, we want to use the same strategy—giving them a few important landmarks to understand the context without requiring them to be an expert.

How much do you know about body temperature? After falling through the ice on a stream while skiing, Anna Bågenholm spent 40 minutes in the freezing water, breathing from an air pocket while rescuers strove to reach her. Then she lost consciousness, her breathing and blood circulation stopped, and she spent another 40 minutes underwater before she was pulled out from under the ice.

"Normal body temperature is 37° Celsius. Hypothermia begins to set in at about 35°C. When Anna arrived at the hospital, her temperature was 13.7°C. No one that cold had ever lived."

A few simple landmarks give us all we need to understand this extraordinary rescue and survival story. We get a sense of what normal and dangerous temperatures are, and we understand that this scenario is far off the map. Even American readers unfamiliar with the Celsius scale can follow this story, and they'll actually have more pertinent information than if we'd just told them that Anna came to the hospital chilled to 56.6 degrees Fahrenheit. (Anna survived and spent some years working as a radiologist at the hospital that saved her. She continued skiing.)

Here's another example of a scale that tells you everything you need to know, and how it might be delivered first by an average doctor and then by a doctor who's great at communicating.

"A normal platelet count ranges from 150,000 to 450,000 platelets per microliter of blood. Your recent blood work showed that your platelet count is 40,000. That's way too low."	"Normal scores for platelet counts are expressed in thousands, and they range between 150 to 450. At 50, we won't let you travel. At 10, you're at risk for spontaneous bleeding. You're at 40."

There are two things that work well in the example on the right. First, the scale is simplified, shrunk down so it's easier to understand. As patients, we don't need to know exactly how many platelets are in a microliter. We need to know how our own count relates to our health.

Second, there are meaningful landmarks in both directions.

We don't just learn that we're "below normal"—we learn that our count is so low we can't travel. And we know that it could drop still further, leading to additional risks. All this orients us to a situation that's serious but where intervention can still help—something we don't get clearly from the first example.

Use Existing Maps When Possible

These first two scenarios were simple enough that just a few numbers helped us get our bearings. Our audience can remember a few relevant numbers, but not a whole map.

But what if we're trying to understand something a bit bigger—say, how human life on Earth fits into the history of the universe?

It turns out we already have an existing way to map out time—and if we put natural history on this scale, we can understand many profound things.

Modern humans first appeared 200,000 years ago—a very recent addition to the universe. The Big Bang occurred an estimated 13.8 billion years ago.

Suppose the history of the universe spanned the 24 hours of a single day. The Big Bang happens precisely at midnight. For a long time, nothing happens. 12 hours pass, then 16. At about 4:10 p.m., our sun comes to life in the midst of a cloud of dust and the planets start forming around it. 5 minutes later, the Earth appears and starts to cool.
    Single-celled life appears on Earth by 5:30 p.m. Vertebrates don't arrive until late that evening at 11:09 p.m. Dinosaurs and the first mammals appear around 11:37 p.m. T. rex shows up at 11:52, with 8 minutes left in the day, but disappears when an asteroid hits a minute later.
    The entire history of humankind doesn't even take up the final second.

Humans are very good at understanding time instinctively—provided the scale is small enough.* No matter how many strong landmarks we put on the scale of geologic time, it will never be as intuitive as the hours, minutes, and seconds of a day, something we experience every day.

This map gives us the key to understanding not only how brief and precious is our own existence, but also all sorts of facts about the history of existence. We understand more about dinosaurs, organisms, planets, and the solar system.

We can add new facts to the scale based on what interests us. When did the moon form? About 9 minutes after Earth, at 4:24 p.m. When did horseshoe crabs show up? At 11:24 p.m., way before *T. rex*. How old are the Appalachian Mountains? 50 minutes old, older even than horseshoe crabs. The Himalayas have only been around 5 minutes, which is why they're so much higher and more jagged. As soon as we have a landscape—or, in this case, a time scape—we can hang all sorts of numbers on it.

---

* Anything from a day to a year is typically in the right range—we experience these measurements of time repeatedly and get a sense of how they work. We went with a day for this example. On the other end, Carl Sagan did a famous Cosmic Calendar that shrank the history of the universe down to a calendar year.

Build a Scale Model You Can Work With

Model trains. Dollhouses. Legos. All these things are the opposite of overwhelming and intimidating. Train schedules, housework, Gantt charts are chores. But when everything exists on a small scale, laid out on the floor where our parents can step on them and make funny/angry sounds, we enjoy playing with these things.

But they're not just fun—a good scale model can be deeply instructive. Aircraft design is so complex that functionality can't be predicted from physics alone. Designers need to test scale models of planes inside wind tunnels to view the subtle interactions between, say, wing shape and position and fuselage.

This chapter will examine how to create models that are complex enough to allow people to generate new insights and make complex trade-offs.

Here's an interactive model that deals with controversial policy issues, using a technique we discussed in the previous chapter—using an existing map of time (in the last chapter, a 24-hour day, in the next example, a calendar year) to understand something much larger. The example assumes a typical, 5-day, 40-hour workweek.

In 2018, the U.S. government spent $68 billion on food and nutrition assistance and $149 billion on higher education. The federal government spends a lot of money on food stamps and higher education.

Instead of giving the government a fraction of each paycheck throughout the year, imagine that you pay your yearly taxes up front. When you start working on January 1, every dime you make goes toward paying your taxes; when you're done, you get to keep 100% of your earnings.

Everything you earn in the first 2 weeks of January goes toward Social Security payments. It takes another 2 weeks to pay off Medicare and Medicaid. Starting February 1, you spend 5 days paying down interest on the national debt. You spend a week and a half working for national defense. Then essentially everything you know and associate with government is paid for out of that last week and a half—meat inspectors, flight controllers, CDC biologists, federal judges, FBI agents, diplomats. Out of the whole year, about 6 hours goes to SNAP, 12 minutes to the national parks, and about 2 hours to NASA.

Putting the government's budget on a calendar scale lets us not only measure these goals against each other but also feel things about them. We don't have an innate reaction to $117 billion or $1.2 trillion in a budget, but we know what it means to work for 8 hours instead of 2 weeks.

It also makes it personal. An education budget of $149 billion might sound high, but if we're willing to spend a few hours tutoring every year, we might also be willing to spend a few days of our earnings paying professionals to teach our fellow Americans. If we can spend a few hours at a soup kitchen, we can spend a single day feeding others at scale—especially when we learn that the majority of the money goes to feed kids. Most Americans love Social Security—but seeing that it's two whole weeks of work might lead us to ask how we could slice that down.

You're probably already imagining other arguments that could be played out in this scale model—depending on your knowledge and ideology. You might even be feeling optimistic about making some attacks, or apprehensive about defending some positions. That's a good thing. It means that you're engaging with these large-scale, seemingly immovable problems in a concrete way, and feeling emotionally invested.

If you're extra-creative, you might even be thinking of tinkering with the model itself. What if you find other revenue sources? What if you model it differently for different players—after all, not everyone is in the same tax bracket, and some people don't make their money from working.

That's a feature, not a bug. In game design, it's called "flexibility" and "expandability." Your base model, the first scenario, is simplified, in order to let you explore a few key dynamics—in this case trading off between budget priorities. You play out a few things to get it right. But once you grasp it, you can try all sorts of variants to explore other factors.

The award-winning board game Settlers of Catan has this property. The original game requires players to acquire the mix of resources that are necessary to grow a village and turn it into a city, but for experienced players, there are several expansions that bring additional dynamics into play. One adds sea travel and trade. Another makes you defend your trade routes against the barbarians. If your first scale model is solid enough, it will become a gift that keeps on giving.

Speaking of which, there's one more move that can add another dimension to your microcosm game: flexible analogies.

The first scenario was a fairly direct miniaturization.

But how would you translate the following study on workplace productivity?

This example is drawn from Stephen Covey's *The 8th Habit*: When workers in an organization were polled, "only 37% said they have a clear understanding of what their organization is trying to achieve and why . . . Only 1 in 5 was enthusiastic about their team's and organization's goals. Only 1 in 5 workers said they have a clear 'line of sight' between their tasks and their team's and organization's goals . . . Only 15% felt that their organization fully enables them to execute key goals . . . Only 20% fully trusted the organization they work for."

It's hard, right? We don't know what the organization does, and it may in fact be many different things that would be hard to

| "When workers in an organization were polled, "only 37% said they have a clear understanding of what their organization is trying to achieve and why . . . Only 1 in 5 was enthusiastic about their team's and organization's goals. Only 1 in 5 workers said they have a clear 'line of sight' between their tasks and their team's and organization's goals . . . Only 15% felt that their organization fully enables them to execute key goals . . . Only 20% fully trusted the organization they work for." | "Imagine if you were coaching 11 people on a soccer team, and only 4 of your players knew which goal they were aiming for. Only 2 of your players cared about which goal was theirs. Only 2 players knew their position and how it related to the team overall. Only 2 players really trusted the coaches and team owners. Only 2 players thought that they were given enough support to play their position as well as they knew they could. Most of your players would be aimlessly kicking a ball around the field." |

miniaturize all together. But with a good analogy, Stephen Covey was able to build a model that worked.

The office did not produce soccer. But all the results apply to team dynamics we could easily observe in a soccer team. You don't have to be a deep fan or supporter to have feelings and reactions when you imagine this dysfunctional team. People running in the wrong direction, kicking willy-nilly, ignoring their coaches, lacking the training or support to play their positions—it's a mess and an embarrassment. And we could expect the organization to have some analogous losses to its ability to function. The soccer analogy just makes it instantly visible, while the problems of a dysfunctional workplace are more slippery and insidious.

What other systems may we want to model in miniature? We could shrink the price of an airline ticket to the scale of $10 and see how much of that goes to employees (pilots, flight attendants, mechanics, administrators, everyone who makes the plane run), how much to fuel, how much to buy and maintain the planes, and how much to purchase those annoying ads where someone with perfect body parts is vacationing at a lovelier spot than you. If we wanted to imagine a different era, we might model the day of a hunter-gatherer or, for that matter, a lion, against our own—how much time is spent hunting, sleeping, fighting, playing? We could model an indie band's revenue and see whether touring, endorsements, or record sales are keeping them afloat.

Whatever the system, a scale model makes all the complex dynamics much more approachable, and lets us bring the numbers into one place where they all make sense. Here, we can get the conversation started. Here, we can make the numbers count.

Epilogue: The Value of Numbers

We set out to write this book for two kinds of people: "I am *not* a numbers person" people, and "I *am* a numbers person" people. Those at least are the labels we apply to ourselves.

But we suspect we're wrong about the labels we have chosen for ourselves.

You might have thought of yourself as a numbers person when you started this book. But the line may have blurred; for example, you might be a little shaken and sobered that you misestimated so much of what is made clear through the use of translations. Perhaps you always thought of nerve impulses as fast, or the NEA budget as large, or the Rockies as high (K2 is laughing at you right now . . .).

If you thought of yourself as not a numbers person, perhaps you've been somewhat reassured that none of us is . . . and genuinely excited by some of the translations. Perhaps you've found yourself telling one to your spouse or your kids—avoiding (most of) the eye rolls you expected from a numbers discussion, especially, when you talked about the hummingbird and the clapping game.

Once we're there, once we're speaking about a well-executed number translation, numbers not only make sense, they feel sort of effortless. People who don't know the metric system can understand a tumor the size of a grape—that's 3 cm, just put into human terms. People who don't know astronomical units can understand that if our solar system is the size of a quarter, we need to walk a whole soccer field to get to the next solar system, another tiny quarter out in the grass.

We've seen sixth graders (11-year-olds) get excited about knowing the difference between a million seconds and a billion seconds. A million seconds is 12 days from now, the next pizza day in the cafeteria. A billion seconds is 32 years, unfathomably far off in the future (the 11-year-old will be 43!), past high school and college and first jobs and over the horizon into the boring years of chauffeuring kids and heart attacks.

Numbers are so inherently far from our experience that even when we think we've mastered them, they can still slip by us. Venture capitalists specializing in tech are awash in numbers, atop the intersection of two fields, tech and finance, so math-heavy they each come with their own vocabulary. You think they'd know their numbers, right?

But in 2002, they were collectively investing in start-ups at a rate that assumed they'd create over a trillion dollars in market value in 10 years. That might have sounded reasonable—a decade is a long time. But when a *Fortune* magazine writer pointed out that this meant "1 eBay every 10 days till 2010," the realization hit them. *"Naah, not going to happen."*

It's not that the VCs didn't have the information available, that they didn't know their math, or that they didn't care about their investments. It's just that they're human, and any human can be exuberant about the future and get lost at sea when it comes to large and complex numbers. It doesn't take a prodigy or breakthrough to make the right translation—just someone asking the right question in the right way.

We know that complex numbers, like complex language, can distort the truth, as Darrell Huff proved with his 1954 classic *How to Lie with Statistics*. It was loaded with tips to spot statistical distortion. But if people only look for the lies, they tend to doubt everything. We're no wiser to assume everyone's lying than that everyone's telling the truth.

Far more useful is the ability to draw out the truth itself, which lets us not only spot the lies but also start conversations around mutual truths. If we can practice making numbers into real things—Krispy Kreme donuts, populations of cities, deaths from a disease—then we don't have to automatically trust or distrust. We can sort for ourselves.

Good translations can build mutual ground. People may argue with fervor about the $148 million NEA budget, but when a translation shows that this means each of us is paying about 25 cents a year, the argument is bound to get a lot more reasonable. If we break out the major budget expenses into how many weeks we're each working to pay them off, we get a sober look at what's really costing us, and where it might be worth cutting back or investing more.

Many of the best moments in life are great because they make space for wonder.

Numbers, with good translations, can slake our curiosity . . . or stoke it. "What would it be like to be a hummingbird?" we might wonder. "We'd have 50 times our metabolism" means very little. "We'd have to drink more than a can of Coke every 60 seconds" tells us a lot, and lets us wonder at the vast differences among creatures.

One thing that we didn't appreciate when we started writing a book about numbers was how often sourcing numbers for this book would leave us feeling an emotion that we most commonly associate with nature and religion but that we really don't spend much time experiencing at all . . .

Awe.

The numbers in this book awed us. A milk jug and some ice cubes made us feel in awe of the scarce supply of drinkable water on a planet that seems to be awash in water. The vast journeys that ants can make, while guided by a natural GPS system better than anything our satellites can produce, awed us: a demonstration of the ingenuity of nature. Clapping 4 times in a second awed us—it helped us appreciate the extraordinary quickness of athletes. We were brought up short by the inequities of society when we imagined a set of 100 apartments divided unfairly among 100 people. Our quarters in a soccer field put us in awe of the vastness in space.

Once we're awed, we never think of the things that awed us in the same way again. Awe rearranges our priorities in the world; it also works on us internally, making us feel more humble, more centered, melting away our petty problems for a while. Long enough, when we step back into the ordinary, for us to make a choice about what's really worth focusing on. And what things, larger than ourselves, we want to be a part of.

You are not a numbers person because you weren't built to be one. None of us was. We don't naturally see numbers more than 5; we can't do complex operations in our head.

But you are a numbers person because you can get excited by the things that numbers describe. For anything you care to do, plan, or imagine, there's a number attached to it, and for every number there's some translation that will allow you and others to intuitively understand and feel that number.

Whether you are a coach trying to prepare your team for an unnaturally challenging opponent, an environmental activist trying to convince a town of the importance of water conservation, a manager trying to motivate everyone from factory workers to VPs to tackle a seemingly boring supply-chain problem, or an English teacher trying to convince young readers that they really can finish that long novel if they take it a day at time, numbers have a place in your work. You will have more success if you are able to translate your numbers so everyone around you can understand and engage.

We believe the world becomes a better place when we use numbers more often and more wisely. Counter to conventional practice, that probably won't involve squeezing more statistics on a page. In fact, it will often mean using fewer digits but with more impact. We believe in numbers not as background, not as decorations, but as central points, with profound stories to tell. We believe in numbers, deeply. We believe in making them count.

APPENDIX: Making Your Numbers User-Friendly

The gold standard for user-friendly is small, whole numbers.

Fractions fail Rule #1: Simpler is better. They take working numbers and force people to do math to interpret them.

Unless fractions involve only simple numbers under 5 they are too complex. That's why people usually convert them to a decimal if they can.

Still, decimals fail Rule #2: Concrete is better. Because they deal with parts and fractions our brains treat them as artificial and unreal. Unless you're reporting a batting average or the cents on a dollar, don't use them (and if you're reporting cents on a dollar, you probably want to round).

Percentages are a strong choice if you have lots of numbers to compare. Responses on a survey. Probabilities of rain on various days. Forecasts of sales of various options.

However, **percentages suffer because they are not sufficiently concrete**. People make more logical mistakes when reasoning from percentages than whole numbers. If you want to keep the comparative precision of percentages but avoid the limits of intangibility, try the "village of 100" strategy: make a "basket" of 100 of whatever you're sampling, and convert the percentages to whole numbers. You're eliminating the denominator without losing any information. **Whole numbers are generally meaningful and strong**, and when properly rounded they are the easiest numbers for our brains to process. Aim for simple, clean, whole numbers unless you're catering to learned cultural tools.

The rules above have an exception: Culture gives us a few tools that we learn so well over time that they trump the rules. Always use the local measuring system when you can. Don't take away baseball fans' clunky 3-digit decimal because they love their batting averages. Similarly don't take away the baker's fractionated measuring cups with 1/4 or 1/3 or their measuring spoons with 1/4 and 1/8.

Rule #1: Round with Enthusiasm

Remember that our audience is busy and has a lot to think about. They want numbers that let them see the big picture and make sense of things—not numbers that require extra chores.

When we heave a nonuser-friendly number across the room to our audience, we are dumping extra work on them. Even if it's simple work, we're wasting their time, energy, and patience. Remember how George A. Miller described our mental workspace as containing 7 slots (plus or minus 2). Just one complex number in our slide deck, let's say, *$85.37 plus 24% value-added tax*, could easily steal our processing capacity for the whole workspace.

Every moment spent trying to understand a number makes it harder to grasp the big picture. Complex, textured numbers—880,320 liters, 43% fewer pages, 267.9 kilometers—don't clarify because they force us to deal with unnecessary complexity. Simplify your numbers—a million liters, 50% fewer pages, 300 kilometers—and give your audience the gift of enough spare capacity that they have space left over to see the big picture.

Hard, slow to comprehend, complicated, user-hostile	Rounded, quick to grasp, simple
0.34165	A little over 3 out of 10
2/49	About 1 out of 25
Four score and seven years ago	Four score and seven years ago*†
483 × 9.79	500 × 10
64% of Boomers said the Beatles were the best rock group of all time	2 out of every 3 Boomers named the Beatles as the best of all time
87.387 kilometers	Slightly under 90 kilometers
4,753,639,000,000	Almost 5 trillion

* Don't quibble with brilliance. The day we become "one for the ages," we get to disregard the rules too.

---

† Lincoln, if we understood the language of his time, is probably making things concrete for his audience. In that era's standard translation of the Bible (King James), Psalm 90:10 described the length of a man's life as three score and ten years (70 years). Lincoln was subtly reminding the crowd that the United States had already outlasted its founders and had already beaten their own likely time on earth.

A quick digression for *Jeopardy* fans: "The answer is: "Psalm 90 is the one song attributed to this leader, who is also credited with a major set of five books?" Question: "Who was Moses?" *In gratitude, Alex.*

Rule #2: Concrete Is Better

Use whole numbers, not too many. Preferably small. Whenever possible, count real things, not decimals or fractions. By far the easiest thing to process are whole numbers under 10. Best are 1–5, the things we can count on one hand and *subitize* at a glance, but anything we can count on the fingers of both hands is solid.

Fractions are generally awful because the complexity takes you out of the flow of things. Quick, how would you like 6/19 of that pie? (Our recommendation is to hold out for 19/37!) Converting a fraction to a decimal eliminates some of the math—no more weird denominators— but still isn't intuitive. "Would you like .316 pies?"

If you hear that 8.33% of eggs from a certain hatchery are rotten, it feels abstract. One egg out of your carton of a dozen? That's real. But if you go further up to 12 rotten eggs out of a gross (144), your number starts to get lost in the crowd again. Once you go up to something both large and arbitrary—say, 3,098 eggs out of 37,176—it's nearly meaningless.

If you can't get to a whole number, go with a percent. 32% is much better than .32, because it *looks* whole, and, unlike decimals, we use percentages colloquially. "A 50% chance," not "a .5 probability."

So, to recap, choose common language when possible: "One out of three" instead of "1/3." Choose percentages over decimals: "33%" instead of ".33." And also choose percentages over complex fractions: "41%" instead of "7/17."

Too many decimals, percentages, and fractions	More concrete, clear use of whole numbers and amounts
Why don't you give me 2 times as many, at 50% of the cost?	Give me twice as many at half the cost?
Give me 50% of the cookies	Give me 3 cookies
A 600% increase	7 times bigger
1/33 students; 3% of the students	About 2 students in this classroom
.001%	1 out of 100 thousand
12.5% of a pizza; 1/8 of a pizza	Give me a slice!
12.5% of women will develop breast cancer	1 out of 8 women will develop breast cancer
A 95% dip in ticket sales	For every 100 seats we used to sell, we're now selling 5

Rule #3: Defer to Expertise

Speak your audience's language. If your audience knows how to work with one kind of number, use it. The fundamental goal of translation is to be understood. We normally wouldn't advise a three-decimal-place probability to express the odds of success, but baseball fans will recognize "batting .300" better than "30% hit rate" or "gets a hit about 3 out of 10 times."

So give them what they know, use the form most familiar to your audience. To a layperson, an exponent isn't a normal part of daily life and shouldn't be part of their statistics. But to a scientist who works with powers of 10 on a regular basis, scientific notation makes numbers simpler. Shoppers know sales discounts, baseball

fans know batting averages, pollsters know percentage points.
Give experts the form they understand.

For the general population	Defer to the expertise of your audience
1 out of 4 times	For a baseball audience: .253 batting average
2 minutes	For a horse-racing audience: 2:03.98
Almost a 1 in 5 chance	For a horse-betting audience: 3 to 13 odds
3 inches	For a construction audience: 2-7/8 in
This shirt is cheaper	For a shopping audience: 35% off
A minor earthquake	For an Angelino: 3.3 on the Richter scale
An average-size apartment in NYC	For a real-estate agent (or a New Yorker who moves frequently): 775 square feet
1 trillion	For a scientific audience: 1×10^{12}

ENDNOTES

Endnotes provide more detail about our sources and the research behind the book. But for more details on the sources and calculations, visit our webnote page: heathbrothers.com/mnc/webnotes.

xii **Subitizing:** Pronounced "SUE-bih-tizing," from *subitus*, the Latin word for "immediate" or "sudden," is the term used to describe people's ability to "rapidly and unambiguously" recognize small quantities of up to 3 or 4 (https://bit.ly/3dmWH2H) and sometimes up to 5. Consider the immediate recognition of numbers on a pair of dice. Humans are not unique in this ability. Similar abilities have been observed in other species, ranging from primates (https://bit.ly/3e5OL5m) to bees and cuttlefish (https://bit .ly/3doWMDf).

xii **The supply of numbers with names runs dry:** There is evidence that cultures don't develop numbers over 5 until they reach a sufficient level of complexity in terms of material possessions—you don't need to count if you don't have stuff to count. For example, Overmann studied a sample of 33 contemporary hunter-gatherer societies whose number systems had been described by anthropologists. Of the cultures without much stuff (simple hunter-gatherer societies), 0 out of 7 had numbers over 5, but 17 out of 26 of the more complex cultures had elaborate number systems, including one or two bases (for example, in addition to the base-10 system modern culture has adopted, various cultures have frequently adopted base-5 and base-20 systems—humans have 5 fingers on each hand and 20 toes and fingers in all). Strong material cultures also tended to have physical devices (for example, tally sticks or beads) to aid counting (Overmann, 2013, p. 28); "the Pomo used stringed beads and tally sticks of various sizes, with a small stick equivalent to 80 beads and five tallies 'equivalent to one of the large sticks or four hundred beads'" (p. 25). Since humans existed in simple hunter-gatherer societies for most of history, it's a safe assumption that most number systems throughout history have been simple as well. Karenleigh A. Overmann (2013), "Material Scaffolds in Numbers and Time." *Cambridge Archaeological Journal*, 23:1, 19–39.

xii **"Yeah, but I meant, like, lots-lots":** (Yes, we did just footnote a joke.) These scenarios are funny to imagine, but they are based on serious dilemmas. Anthropologists have noted that societies without numbers faced disadvantages relative to other societies ("Both the Ainu and Korak were described being cheated in trade through a disadvantage of quantification skills": Overmann, p. 28). They were also disadvantaged relative to challenges in the natural environment: one anthropologist has argued that climate instability forced cultures to develop number systems to count food items and seeds to survive long winters without starvation (see Divale, 1999, paper cited by Overmann, p. 25). Overmann cites the observations of anthropological fieldworkers who found that the Aleut had named February "last stored food" month and March "foregoing hunger" month (that is, "giving up hunger" month). As food ran out in February and March, the Aleut would chew on "relatively inedible" things such as skins or thongs.

xiii **First, systems for counting; then numbers; then mathematics:** Counting alone produces huge social advantages. Not addition or subtraction— just knowing the number of seeds in storage or the number of days a journey takes. In terms of counting, a set of well-known rules for composing higher-order numbers allows people to count higher, but a society needs linguistic infrastructure for guiding this. (For example, Chinese numbers are easier than English. In Chinese, 37 is "three tens seven"; English speakers have to learn the novel word "thirty" instead of the more straightforward "three tens.") But counting was the initial huge innovation. Compared with counting, calculus and geometry are of trivial utility.

The preference for whole numbers may be linked to a human predisposition for counting with our fingers. The first counting device is almost inevitably the body, most specifically fingers. (Thus number systems tend to be base-5 or base-10, though occasionally an especially canny culture will use a system base-20: fingers and toes.) Anthropologists have noted that counting with fingers is cross-culturally "ubiquitous" (an admission that anthropologists, who celebrate the diversity of cultural life, are not wont to make casually). Finger and hand movements are controlled by the same area in the brain as basic number functions (Overmann, 2013, pp. 21–22).

Being able to move the fingers helps people learn about numbers, and when researchers give people a task with their hands that is unrelated to counting, it becomes harder for people to simultaneously count.

xiii **Spend $50,000:**
After winning a million: $1,000,000 ÷ $50,000 per day = 20 days.
After willing a billion: $1,000,000,000 ÷ $50,000 per day = 20,000 days.
20,000 days ÷ 365 days per year = 54.8 years.

xv ***Guinness Book of World Records:*** First published in 1955, the definitive, world-renowned reference book was originally created to help people settle bar bets: https://bit.ly/3diqcmq

xv **Box: McDonald's advertising budget vs. USDA 5 A Day**
In the documentary *Super Size Me*, Morgan Spurlock illustrates the vast difference between the McDonald's advertising budget ($1.4 billion global) and the USDA program budget for promoting fruits and veggies ($2 million). How much of the McDonald's $1.4 billion is spent in the United States? About 40% of the stores are in the United States, but the U.S. advertising market is larger than that that of other countries, so let's assume that half of their global ad spend is in the States ($700 million). That means that for every $1 spent by the USDA on their 5 A Day message about fruits and veggies, McDonald's spends $350.

If we were to reimagine these numbers today, we might be pleasantly surprised to discover that McDonald's has downsized its budget to a mere $366 million (https://bit.ly/3sqxaKk) and the USDA spends roughly the same $2 million (as reported by a USDA budget officer), giving us a ratio of 183:1. That means McDonald's is only showing an ad every other day (compared to once a year for the USDA), instead of every single day. Progress!

For more, see heathbrothers.com/mnc/webnotes.

xvi **"psychophysical numbing":** A phenomenon studied by psychologist Paul Slovic in which he observes that as numbers increase, the ability we have to emotionally respond to the number decreases. For example, when we hear about the tragic suffering of one person, we feel it deeply, but when confronted with the suffering of thousands, it becomes abstract, and our ability to empathize is diminished. Sobering fact: the reduction in empathy begins as soon as we get past 1 person and begin thinking about 2 instead. Paul Slovic and Daniel Västfjäll (2013): "The More Who Die, The Less We Care: Psychic Numbing and Genocide," *Behavioural Public Policy,* ed. Adam Oliver (Cambridge: Cambridge University Press). (https://bit.ly/3mRCMMH)

xx **"the Curse of Knowledge":** The curse of knowledge has been studied in psychology and economics. For a discussion of the phenomenon, see Chip Heath and Dan Heath (2007), *Made to Stick: Why Some Ideas Survive and Others Die* (New York: Random House), pp. 19–21. The same skills that help us arrive at an answer get in the way when it comes time to share that answer with others. This phenomenon was originally identified and labeled by Colin Camerer, George Loewenstein, and Martin Weber (1989), "The Curse of Knowledge in Economic Settings: An Experimental Analysis" *Journal of Political Economy* 97:5 pp. 1232–54. (https://bit.ly/33PMvdM)

3 **Circle each number and then look above and below:** Shout-out to Andy Craig and Dave Yewman, masters of sticky ideas, who told us about this exercise they do with all the presenters they coach.

4 **Perspectives Engine:** in their study, Jake Hofman and Dan Goldstein found that perspective phrases cut the magnitude of errors in half, as seen in Figure 5 of Christopher Riederer, Jake M. Hofman, and Daniel G. Goldstein (2018), "To Put That in Perspective: Generating Analogies That Make Numbers Easier to Understand," *Proceedings of the 2018 CHI Conference on Human Factors in Computing Systems.* (https://bit.ly/32j0Pum)

The Perspectives Engine team found that offering perspectives substantially improves people's ability "to recall measurements they have read, estimate ones they have not, and detect errors in manipulated measurements." The ability of some subjects to retain information increased by as much as 15% (which sounds small-ish but in a high-school or college

For more, see heathbrothers.com/mnc/webnotes.

class that might represent a letter grade and a half). Pablo J. Barrio, Daniel Goldstein, and Jake Hofman (2016), "Improving Comprehension of Numbers in the News," *Proceedings of the 2016 CHI Conference on Human Factors in Computing Systems*. (https://bit.ly/3x1Yn9R)

4 **Pakistan = 2 Californias:** Square miles of Pakistan: 340,000 (https://bit.ly/3nauAqX), square miles of California: 164,000 (https://bit.ly/3ajyqc1) 164,000 × 2 = 328,000.

7 **Box: Gallon jug, ice cubes, drops**
According to *National Geographic*, only .025% of the world's fresh water is both usable and accessible (https://on.natgeo.com/32Qfttv). If we represent all the water in the world as a gallon jug, the total volume of fresh water (including what's locked away in glaciers) is only about 2.5% of the gallon, or 94 milliliters. Homemade ice cubes are around 30 ml (personal cooking lab notes). This gives us 3 refreshing ice cubes. However, if only 1% of the fresh water on earth is accessible in non-icy form, we're left with less than 1 ml—about 6 drops melting off each of the cubes. The California Bureau of Reclamation has a larger-scale illustration of this (https://on.doi.gov/35Xij1u), but we find the smaller scale model more visually impactful.

8 **Box: Scale of Mars volcano Olympus Mons**
According to the *Encyclopedia Britannica* (https://bit.ly/2Q2Ktnn), at 14 miles (22 km) tall, Olympus Mons is more than 2 times taller than any earthly peak. Commercial airliners cruise safely at an altitude of 31,000 to 38,000 feet (https://bit.ly/3xgVYs3), but Mons soars far beyond that at 74,000 feet tall. At such an altitude, a commercial airliner would hit air so thin that the oxygen would be insufficient to fuel the engines, and the trip would end badly. At 435 miles across (https://bit.ly/2Q2Ktnn), Mons is slightly wider than Arizona (https://bit.ly/32n5kEh). A 747 jet cruising at 550 mph would take more than 45 minutes just to fly alongside Mons, and the peak would loom on the horizon for far longer. How long do you think it would take an average skier (https://bit.ly/3alEkJP) to get from peak to base? Trick question—the skier would die from lack of oxygen long before even the halfway mark.

For more, see heathbrothers.com/mnc/webnotes.

9 **Box: More CEOs named "James" than women**
In 2018, the *New York Times* reported that there were more Fortune 500 CEOs named James than there were women in those positions (https://nyti.ms/3tuyL37). As of 2021, there are more women (https://cnn.it/32olxsU) than Jameses (progress!), but note that the translation would still shock even if we had to list the top 3 male names to exceed the number of female CEOs—for example, "more CEOs named 'Robert,' 'Scott,' or 'James' than women." With Jameses making up only 1.682% of the population and women making up 50.8% (https://bit.ly/3uSPQE4), the problem is glaringly obvious. Maybe we need to name more daughters James.

10 **Box: Black and White applicants with criminal records**
In her brilliantly designed study, Devah Pager (https://bit.ly/3svUiqS) demonstrates that while a criminal record impacts the callback rates of all job applicants, a White applicant with a felony conviction is more likely to be considered for a job than a Black applicant with no criminal record.

11 **Box: LeBron James, point-scoring machine**
While LeBron's lifetime total of over 35,000 points (https://bit.ly/3x2D4EV) sounds impressive, when you take the time to spread those points out over his 1,300 games, the impact really hits home. His 27 points per game (https://bit.ly/3x2CA1z) sustained over a career-spanning 18 years and counting is truly mind-blowing.

12 **Box: America, world leader in civilian firearms**
According to the Small Arms Survey (https://bit.ly/3uVBBP2), the 400 million civilian-owned arms in America far outnumber the 330 million citizens—by 70 million. In fact, despite making up only 4 percent of the world's population, Americans own about 46 percent of the entire global stock of civilian firearms (https://wapo.st/3gjpIhG). If we distribute these 70 million surplus weapons among the entire active-duty military population of 1,346,000 (https://bit.ly/2Qy8xOC), each soldier, sailor, pilot, and accountant would end up with 52 firearms.

13 **Box: Muhammad Yunus, father of microlending**
Based on this experience, in 1976 Yunus founded Grameen Bank to strategically loan money to the very, very poor. He won the Nobel Peace Prize

For more, see heathbrothers.com/mnc/webnotes.

in 2006 (https://bit.ly/2RA4oKw). This anecdote comes from Muhammad Yunus (1999), *Banker to the Poor: Micro-Lending and the Battle Against World Poverty* (New York: Perseus Books).

14 **Box: National debt per person**
According to the U.S. Government Accountability Office, the national debt rose to $27 trillion in September 2020 (https://bit.ly/3gijgaN). While that number is impossible to imagine, when divided up among the 330 million American citizens, it represents about $82,000 per person. That's lots, but not *lots-lots*, like a trillion.

15 **Box: Prototypical customer**
This example is based on a case study from Chip Heath and Dan Heath (2007): *Made to Stick: Why Some Ideas Survive and Others Die* (New York: Random House). The case followed Melissa Studzinski, the brand manager of Hamburger Helper (see pp. 126–28).

18 **The Magical Number 7:** First published in 1956, in a remarkably conversational paper, George A. Miller offers evidence suggesting that our human brains can retain and manipulate around 7 independent pieces of information at a time without a high risk of error. George A. Miller (1956), "The Magical Number Seven, Plus or Minus Two: Some Limits on Our Capacity for Processing Information," *Psychological Review* 63(2): pp 81–97. (https://bit.ly/3x6qsN2)

19 **The value of the new A&W burger:** As told by A&W CEO Alfred Taubman in his memoir. (https://bit.ly/3mTKQfV) A. Alfred Taubman (2007), *Threshold Resistance: The Extraordinary Career of a Luxury Retailing Pioneer.* (New York: Harper Business).

20 **Rounding, Frick collection experiment:** Jake Hofman and Daniel Goldstein (2021), "Round Numbers Can Sharpen Cognition." Preprint available at the Open Science Framework. (https://osf.io/4n7sk/)

21 **Decimals, fractions, percentages, and ratios—simply don't register as real to our minds:** This has been a long-standing area of research in the field of human decision-making. Thinking in terms of whole objects helps people think through complex math decisions (for example, contingent

For more, see heathbrothers.com/mnc/webnotes.

results from contingent probabilities), but a lack of whole objects leads them to make mistakes even in very simple situations. For example, the "conjunction fallacy" (https://bit.ly/3ggMxmh) finds that in a probabilistic context many people will say the equivalent of "the number of things with needles and green skin is greater than the number of things with needles." People seldom make that mistake when they assign concrete tokens to represent the various labels. Amos Tversky and Daniel Kahneman (1983), "Extensional versus intuitive reasoning: The conjunction fallacy in probability judgment," *Psychological Review*, 90:4, pp. 293–31. Gerd Gigerenzer, Peter M. Todd, and ABC Research Group (1999), *Simple Heuristics That Make Us Smart* (New York: Oxford University Press).

24 **Box: What kind of atoms are most common in the human body**
The periodic table encompasses over 90 naturally occurring elements. Of these, only 11 show up in significant quantities in most living things, and for humans, the big 3 make up the lion's share. We've chosen to focus on the *number* of atoms in the body (https://bit.ly/3tMtUus), but you could also calculate by atomic weight, which will yield a different ordering. (https://bit.ly/3mZyJ0W)

25 **Box: Post-bathroom handwashing by the numbers**
According to a recent YouGov survey, a surprisingly large number of Americans don't wash their filthy paws after using the bathroom at home (https://bit.ly/2Qenp51). It's worth noting that this survey was taken before the COVID-19 pandemic. You may also be interested in knowing that while going to the bathroom, 1 in 2 people use their phone—which happens to carry about 10 times more bacteria than a toilet seat (https://bit.ly/3mWi4ep). We're ~~sure~~ hopeful that a global pandemic changed that for the better.

29 **One survey of 84 cultures:** Kensy Cooperrider and Dedre Gentner (2019), "The career of measurement," *Cognition*, 191. (https://bit.ly/3niVc9h)

29 **The length of the forearm, called a "cubit":** There's actually a great deal of theological debate about whether or not the cubit included the hand. (https://bit.ly/3ebycEX) Archeologists working in the Middle East have identified both "long" and "short" cubits—"long" typically meaning the

For more, see heathbrothers.com/mnc/webnotes.

forearm as well as the hand, while "short" is just the forearm. (https://bit .ly/3ea8FvN)

30 **Collection of social distancing posters:** The *Guardian* posted these (https://bit.ly/2P4QQWI), and links to each are provided in the list below:
1 hockey stick—Canada (https://bit.ly/3tuJ5Z2)
1 tatami mat—Japan (https://bit.ly/3ef4COL)
1 adult gator—Florida (https://cnn.it/3ea8m4l)
1 surfboard—San Diego (https://bit.ly/3epleUb)
1 adult cassowary—North Queensland, Australia (https://bit.ly/2P4QQWI)
1 Michael Jordan—imagine Michael Jordan giving you and your friend an air-five—Virginia basketball court (https://bit.ly/3ay3Uv8)
1 caribou—Yukon, Canada (https://bit.ly/3sqwrsB)
1 bear—Russia (https://bit.ly/3x40KsE)
1 fathom—U.S. Navy (https://bit.ly/3ngV8Xt)
1 alpaca—Ohio county fair (https://bit.ly/32sS553)
1.5 wood chippers—North Dakota (https://bit.ly/3dKlIFw)
2 baguettes—France (https://bit.ly/3xssG9Y)
4 trout or 1 fishing rod—Montana (https://fxn.ws/3axo8Fb)
1 surfboard, or 1-1/2 mountain bikes—Orange County parks department (https://bit.ly/3dGg3QA)
4 koalas—Sydney, Australia (https://bit.ly/3stguC3)
4 Buffalo wings—Buffalo, NY (https://bit.ly/3vdI8F2)
72 pistachios—New Mexico (https://bit.ly/3uZj8Rx)

31 **Box: Pakistan = 2 Californias not 5 Oklahomas**
While the average American may struggle to visualize the area of Pakistan (https://bit.ly/2QDKnlG), let alone locate it on a map, "twice the size of California" provides an easy-to-index comparison. "5 Oklahomas" not only forces readers to visualize a more obscure state but then asks them to do harder math, losing them in the process.

32 **Box: Turkey vs. California**
Turkey is 2 times the size of California. All areas sourced from Wikipedia. Turkey (785,000 square kilometers) is a little less than 2 times California (424,000 square kilometers). New York State (141,000 square kilometers) is almost twice the size of the Republic of Ireland (70,000 square kilome-

ters). The Great Pacific Garbage Patch (1,600,000 square kilometers) covers just over 3 times the area of Spain (506,000 square kilometers).

32 **Box: Australian wildfire comparison**
The Australian wildfire destroyed 186,000 square kilometers (https://bit .ly/3ojwbK2). According to Wikipedia, Japan covers 378,000 square kilometers, Syria is 185,000 square kilometers, the United Kingdom 242,500 square kilometers, and Portugal 92,000 square kilometers. New England (Connecticut, Maine, Massachusetts, New Hampshire, Rhode Island, and Vermont) covers an area that is 186,000 square kilometers, and Washington State covers 185,000 square kilometers.

34 **A chimp, a rhino, and Usain Bolt run a 100-meter dash**
A chimp, a rhino, and the fastest man on earth . . . sounds like the beginning of a joke, but the punch line here is that Usain Bolt—our best—is no match for an animal even as clunky-looking as a rhino. If Bolt runs 100 meters (328 feet) in 8.65 seconds, we can tease out that he travels at .00718 miles per second. Apologies for switching systems, but miles per hour means something to most Americans, while kilometers per hour does not. Multiply that out by the seconds in an hour, and we get a speed of just under 26 miles per hour—just a hair faster than our wildest relative, the chimp, at 25 miles per hour (https://bit.ly/3tpcW53), and way, way behind the rhino's 34 miles per hour. (https://bit.ly/3srCbCj)

34 **Box: Video games market vs. film industry**
While the world's gaze is fixed on the beautiful people of film and music, gamers are quietly laughing all the way to the bank. With revenues reaching $180 billion (https://on.mktw.net/3drI26n), even the $42 billion (pre-COVID-19) global box office record earnings (this gloating *Variety* article did not age well (https://bit.ly/3uVqoxK), and almost $22 billion in music revenues (https://bit.ly/3mZggl0) simply can't compete.

36 **When students whined about being graded on their writing in a math class:** The Grace Hopper quote "I would explain: it was no use trying to learn math unless they could communicate with other people" is from a meticulously researched biography by Kurt W. Beyer (2009), *Grace Hopper and the Invention of the Information Age* (Cambridge: MIT Press) p. 124.

36 **It was 984 feet long:** Grace Hopper's statement "I sometimes think we ought to hang one [of these spools] over every programmer's desk, or around their neck, so they know what they're throwing away when they throw away microseconds" is from the Speaking While Female Speech Bank, "Explaining Nanoseconds: Grace Hopper," accessed March 26, 2021. (https://bit.ly/3mZ4ZkG)

37 **Box: Saving microseconds with Grace Hopper**
Grace Hopper was a master of "show, don't tell." As a public speaker, she was known for handing out foot-long snippets of wire, explaining that they represented a nanosecond, the distance electricity travels in one-billionth of a second. Then, she would extract from her briefcase a spool of wire nearly a thousand feet long—the distance electricity travels in a microsecond. Her 984-foot-long spool was about the length of 3 football fields.

37 **Concreteness helps us understand faster and remember longer:** A 1993 study investigated concreteness as a text feature for engaging reading comprehension, as well as the interest level of readers and their capacity to learn, across 4 text types: persuasion, exposition, literary stories, and narratives. Concrete texts were recalled better in every instance, with magnitudes varying across text types. Mark Sadoski, Ernest T. Goetz, and Maximo Rodriguez (1993), "Engaging Texts: Effects of Comprehensibility, Interest, and Recall in Four Text Types," *Journal of Educational Psychology* 92: pp. 85–95. (https://bit.ly/2RCnnEg)

37 **Cultural products such as proverbs, jokes, folk ballads, and epic sagas:** In his work exploring the mechanisms of memory that underpin counting-out rhymes, ballads, and epics, David Rubin highlights the power of strong concrete imagery to increase the spread and longevity of a song or story. David C. Rubin (1995), *Memory in oral traditions: The cognitive psychology of epic, ballads, and counting-out rhymes.* (Oxford: Oxford University Press).

38 **Tumor table:** PDQ Adult Treatment Editorial Board. Testicular Cancer Treatment (PDQ®): Patient Version. 2019 Apr 9. In: PDQ Cancer Information Summaries [Internet]. Bethesda (MD): National Cancer Institute (US); 2002–. [Figure, Tumor sizes are often measured . . .] Available from: https://bit.ly/3edzyPE

For more, see heathbrothers.com/mnc/webnotes.

39 **Deck of cards serving size:** Source: Center for Disease Control (2008), *Road to Health Toolkit Activities Guide* (U.S. Department of Health and Human Services) pp. 51–52. Available from https://bit.ly/3dsm4Aq.

40 **Box: The container ship *Ever Given***
Besides track runners, who has a clear mental picture of a quarter-mile? The Empire State Building, on the other hand, holds space in our collective minds. *Ever Given*, at 1,312 feet, is longer than the Empire State Building if we remove the thin 200-foot antenna (1,250 feet). Seen like this, we can grasp the magnitude of the ship and how it blocked the Suez Canal. Of note: The container ship (which floats in the ocean) weighs at least 60% as much as the Empire State Building, a building of stone and steel that sits heavily on land. 224,000 tons (https://cnn.it/2PevqGF) vs. 365,000. (https://bit.ly/3gtz3nn)

40 **Supplemental Nutrition Assistance Program:** According to the Center for Budget and Policy Priorities, in fiscal year 2018 the average SNAP household received about $256 a month and the average recipient about $127 a month—about $1.40 per meal (https://bit.ly/3tJVKY9). See part II.

41 **The total amount of the subsidy:** From the SNAP 2018 end-of-year summary. (https://bit.ly/2Q7nd7K)

41 **Meal cost per person:** Nina Hoffman and Sarah Kennedy dished up these recipes in their article "12 Tasty Frugal Meals Under $1.50 Per Serving," on the RecipeLion website. (https://bit.ly/3alhUbs)

42 **Box: Apartments and wealth distribution**
In 2010, the economist Edward Wolff used data from the Federal Reserve to divide Americans into finely grained wealth brackets to establish a clearer picture of the nation's inequality than is offered by census estimates, which typically only measure annual household income (https://bit.ly/3nlpxnt). Recent data from the Federal Reserve indicates that the magnitude of the gap between rich and poor hasn't budged in the decade since Wolff's study, with the top 10% of the country still owning an astounding 70% of the nation's wealth, while the bottom 50% have a mere 2% (https://bit.ly/3eu0mex). Applying our apartment building analogy to 2020, the richest resident would own 31 apartments, the next 9 would

For more, see heathbrothers.com/mnc/webnotes.

have 38 units, the next 40 would have 29 units, and the poorest 50 would be packed into 2 apartments. Edward N. Wolff (2010), "Recent Trends in Household Wealth in the United States: Rising Debt and the Middle-Class Squeeze—an Update to 2007." Levy Economics Institute of Bard College Working Paper No. 589.

42 **Box: Hummingbird metabolism**
For comparison purposes, if we take a hummingbird weighing in at 3 grams, consuming 5 calories a day (https://bit.ly/3x7EuOE), then a "hummingbird" with the proportions of an average American man—weighing 200 pounds (https://bit.ly/3tvn4JG)—would need to take in 150,000 calories a day. Assuming this man-bird hybrid gets 8 hours of sleep each night, that leaves 16 hours a day in which to suck down 67 Cokes every single waking hour.

43 **Vivid things are more colorful and more active:** Vivid things are more immediate. The factors we are postulating to make things more vivid are the same properties that have been studied for social perception, behavior, and choice in construal level theory (https://bit.ly/3sv30FX). The more detailed, or vivid, the image of a thing is in our thoughts, the less psychological distance we experience from it. Yaacov Trope and Nira Liberman (2010), "Construal-level theory of psychological distance" *Psychological Review*. 117:2, pp. 440–63.

43 **Box: Toledo water**
According to Wikipedia, there were 650,000 residents in the Toledo, OH, metro area around the time that officials asked the 500,000 who used the city water supply to stop using tap water because of toxins found in the treatment plant (https://bit.ly/3py11k6). Dividing those restricted by the total population gives us .77, or 77% of Toledo residents, or 3 in 4.

44 **Box: Nearest solar system**
The closest star system to the sun is Proxima Centauri, though in outer space "close" is a relative term. Humans would need to traverse 4.25 light-years, or 40,208,000,000,000 km, to reach it (https://go.nasa.gov/32NRZ8k). Shrinking things to human scale hardly makes things more manageable.

For more, see heathbrothers.com/mnc/webnotes.

If the solar system between the sun and Neptune was shrunk to the size of a quarter—that is, with a diameter of 43 mm (https://bit.ly/3aE8mse)—you'd need to line up 4,500 of those quarters to model the distance between here and Proxima Centauri—around 110 meters, or the length regulation soccer fields (https://fifa.fans/2PrPNjO). See the webnotes for why we didn't define the diameter of the solar system in terms of Pluto's orbit.

46 **Global Village, population 100**
Shrinking the Earth's population of 7.7 billion people to a village of 100 can tell us a lot about the diversity of the human experience—beyond traditional dimensions like geographic origin, religion, and language. For example, 55 of our 100 villagers would live in the urbanized part of the village, while the other 45 would live in the surrounding, rural areas (https://bit.ly/2RUkyP0). Thinking about the world this way can help us understand that we have more in common with the rest of the world than we might think, like when we realize that 65 of the villagers have mobile phones (https://pewrsr.ch/3aEfl4v) and 36 are regular Facebook users (https://bit.ly/3xn0vck). But it can also underscore just how vulnerable our fellow villagers are, with 25 of them facing the loss of drinking water because of climate change (https://bit.ly/3gAX9wj) and 8 in danger of losing their homes to rising sea levels. (https://bit.ly/2Pp3tMo)

49 **Box: A million seconds vs. a billion seconds**
A million seconds is 11.6 days—less than 2 weeks of your life. A billion seconds is 31 years, 8 months, and 5 days—a significant portion of a lifetime.

49 **How long is a million seconds?**
1,000,000 seconds ÷ 60 seconds per minute = 16,666 minutes
16,666 minutes ÷ 60 minutes per hour = 277 hours
277 hours ÷ 24 hours per day = 11.6 days
1,000,000 seconds = about 12 days

49 **How long is a billion seconds?**
1,000,000,000 seconds ÷ 60 seconds per minute = 16,666,666 minutes
16,666,666 minutes ÷ 60 minutes per hour = 277,777 hours
277,777 ÷ 24 hours per day = 11,574 days
11,574 days is how many years?

For more, see heathbrothers.com/mnc/webnotes.

11, 574 days ÷ 365.25 days per year = 31.68 years = 32 years
(Note: 365.25 spreads the leap year every four years across each of those years.)
.68 years × 365.25 days per year = 248.37 days
248.37 days (January–August: 31 + 28 + 31 + 30 + 31 + 30 + 31 + 31) = 8 months, with 5 days left over

49 **Taller than the Eiffel Tower with the Statue of Liberty on top:** The average American is 66.25 inches tall (https://bit.ly/2QRU8go). Three hundred times that is 19,875 inches, or 1,656 feet. The Eiffel Tower is 1,063 feet tall (https://bit.ly/3aB535d), and the Statue of Liberty is 305 feet tall (https://bit.ly/3exyqGD). Stacked, they reach only 1,368 feet—almost another Lady Liberty shorter still.

49 **Box: Engineers trading time for coffee**
If each of 100 engineers on a team takes 10 minutes a day round-trip for a coffee, it adds up to 80 hours per week of time lost. That is the equivalent of the work completed by 2 full-time employees. Engineers make an average of $65,000 a year (https://indeedhi.re/3vlNq1h), so a $15,000 investment in a few new coffee stations would be a relative bargain!

50 **Box: Odds of accidentally dying on any day in England**
What are the odds of dying in an accident in England? According to the UK Office of National Statistics, the population of England and Wales in 2019 was 56.2 million and 3.1 million (https://bit.ly/3vnwS9b), respectively, totaling just shy of 60 million. The estimated number of accidental deaths in England and Wales combined in 2019 was 22.6 thousand (https://bit 49.ly/3sTAyOe). That comes to about 62 accidental deaths per day spread across 60 million people. On any given day, the statistical odds of falling off your perch in England is around 1 in a million.

50 **A unit to measure all types of risk:** Coined in 1989 by Stanford professor Ronald A. Howard, the forefather of modern-day decision analysis, the "micromort" is popularly used to evaluate daily risks. Initially proposed as a convenient unit for measuring most medical risks, the microprobability, or 1 in 1 million probability, in this case of death, becomes a "micromort." A few micromorts listed on Wikipedia in 2021

For more, see heathbrothers.com/mnc/webnotes.

(https://bit.ly/2R2BySH) include: hang gliding (8 micromorts per trip), giving birth (120 micromorts), and living in New York City during the height of the COVID-19 pandemic (50 micromorts per day). Ronald A. Howard (1989), "Microrisks for Medical Decision Analysis," *International Journal of Technology Assessment in Health Care*, 5:3), pp. 357–70. (https://bit.ly/3tUMmRp)

50 **Imagine the entire Harry Potter series:** Harry Potter attracts superfans who read the books, buy wands and costumes, and tally the words in each volume: https://bit.ly/3aCAf3S

Harry Potter and the Sorcerer's Stone: 76,944 words

Harry Potter and the Chamber of Secrets: 85,141 words

Harry Potter and the Prisoner of Azkaban: 107,253 words

Harry Potter and the Goblet of Fire: 190,637 words

Harry Potter and the Order of the Phoenix: 257,045 words

Harry Potter and the Half-Blood Prince: 168,923 words

Harry Potter and the Deathly Hallows: 198,227 words

This brings the total Harry Potter word count to a whopping 1,084,170. Take out *Chamber of Secrets* (it was your favorite!)—it's 85,141 words, and you are left with 999,029.

52 **Box: Effect of cutting NEA funding from the federal budget**
According to the National Endowment for the Arts, the 2016 budget was $148 million out of a total federal budget of $3.85 trillion (https://bit 49.ly/3nogNgr). This represents .004% of the overall budget. According to an algorithm-based word counter (https://bit.ly/3dQscCQ), a typical literary fiction novel averages 90,000 words. Multiply that by .004% and you get . . . 4 words to cut. Easiest editing job ever, but the reader will surely pay the price.

52 **Box: Burning off snack calories**
One M&M contains just shy of 4.5 calories (https://bit 49.ly/3tQW5Z8). While metabolic rate varies by person, according to a science-based calorie counter, the average person burns about .2 calories per step climbed (https://bit.ly/32LC7TF). At this rate, in 2 flights of stairs that M&M would be history. If this makes you feel like taking the stairs instead of the elevator, you're not alone. Calorie counts on labels have been shown to

have little effect on behavior, but translating calories into action has a measurable impact (https://bit.ly/2R0ciwk). The 10-calorie Pringle (https://bit.ly/3nnzMrI) would take a little longer. According to a Harvard Medical School chart (https://bit.ly/3tPqZRK), an average person can burn off 10 calories in 4 minutes of walking at 3.5 mph—a distance of about 695 feet (around 2 football field lengths) . . . a good bit more than we've been walking.

52 **Box: The paper mountain**
According to *Nature*, if you printed only the first page of every academic paper in the Web of Science, the stack would reach almost to the 19,340-foot-high peak of Kilimanjaro (https://go.nature.com/2QXLey5). More curious, perhaps, is that the most-cited papers by far exceed the number of citations for papers detailing much more well-known scientific discoveries.

54 **"Avocados—a stack of nickels":** The average price of an avocado in 2019 was around $2 (https://bit.ly/3eywi1i), or 40 nickels. The U.S. Mint pegs the thickness of a nickel at 1.95 mm (https://bit.ly/2Qrnu5z), which means a stack of 40 of them would measure 78 mm, or 3.07 inches.
$2.00 = 200 cents
200 cents ÷ 5 cents = 40 nickels
40 nickels × 1.95 mm thickness per nickel = 78 mm
78 mm = 3.07 inches

57 **Box: Miniature Mount Everest**
Mount Everest's summit reaches 29,032 feet, making it the tallest mountain on Earth (https://bit.ly/3aA2nob). According to the CDC, Americans average 5 foot 6 (https://bit.ly/2Qy4t1h), making us much, much smaller than Everest but still a great deal bigger than the eraser of a Dixon Ticonderoga pencil, which is about 6 mm tall (https://bit.ly/3sR9Zcc), or a grain of rice, which laid flat is just 2 mm tall (https://bit.ly/3tSLWLk). If a person were the size of an eraser, then Everest would shrink to 103 feet, 11 inches; if each story of an office building is about 14 feet tall (https://bit.ly/3tPo9Mo), that means Everest would reach to between the 7th and 8th floors of a high-rise. If the person gaping up at the mountain was shrunk even further, to the size of a grain of rice, then Everest drops to

For more, see heathbrothers.com/mnc/webnotes.

34 feet, 7 inches—about the height of a generously proportioned two-story house in the suburbs, plus an attic. And then if we shrink the human a step further, to the size of a stack of six cards in a standard deck of playing cards (http://magicorthodoxy.weebly.com/magic-reviews/card-thickness -how-will-these-cards-feel), Everest also shrinks to 29 feet, a more modest version of a two-story house.

57 **If humans shrink to the size of a stack of playing cards:** Bee Red Casino Back playing cards, a common variety, measure 2.78 mm for a stack of 10, which translates to 0.066 inches for a stack of 6 (http://magicorthodoxy .weebly.com/magic-reviews/card-thickness-how-will-these-cards-feel), or 1/1000th the height of an average, 5 foot 6 human. Card thicknesses vary, but so do human heights, and the Bees are near the middle of the pack, so we're comfortable with the 1,000-to-1 scale. Karakoram 2 is 28,251 feet tall (https://bit.ly/3no1MLQ), which at stack-of-cards scale shrinks to just 28 feet, 3 inches, only 9 inches shorter than Everest. The 23,000-foot threshold that so many peaks in the Himalayas soar over (https://bit .ly/3gCAO1n) is still an imposing 27 feet at this scale, and the 14,800-foot-tall Tibetan plateau (https://bit.ly/3aEMM6T) is 14 feet, 7 inches high. Mont Blanc, at 15,771 feet (https://bit.ly/3dMLR6y), is one of the few mountains anywhere else in the world to surpass that level, if only by 11 inches. Colorado's Mount Elbert, the highest peak in the Rockies at 14,443 feet (https://bit.ly/3dRpZ9S), and North Carolina's Mount Mitchell, whose 6,684-foot summit is the tallest east of the Mississippi (https:// bit.ly/3xwuIGb), are both in the shadow of the plateau, shrinking to 14 feet, 5 inches and 6 feet, 8 inches, respectively. Scotland's Ben Nevis, the highest point in the British Islands (https://bit.ly/3nl2NUJ), looks positively shrimpy, its 4,406 feet shrinking down to just 4 feet, 5 inches, no taller than a roadside mailbox. (https://www.usps.com/manage/mailboxes.htm)

For a human at six-card scale: 66 inches ÷ 0.066 inches = 1,000-to-1 scale

K2 is 28,251 feet ÷ 1,000 = 28.25 feet, or 28 feet 3 inches

8,611,000 mm ÷ 838 mm = 10,276 mm, or 33 feet, 8 inches

Himalayas average around 23,000 feet, which converts to an even 23 feet

The Tibetan plateau is around 14,800 feet, which converts to 14.8 feet, or 14 feet, 10 inches

For more, see heathbrothers.com/mnc/webnotes.

Mont Blanc is 15,771 feet, which converts to 15.8 feet, or 15 feet, 9 inches

Mount Elbert is 14,443 feet, which converts to 14.45 feet, or 14 feet, 5 inches

Mount Mitchell is 6,684 feet, which converts to 6.68 feet, or 6 feet, 8 inches

Ben Nevis is 4,406 feet, which converts to 4.41 feet, or 4 feet, 5 inches

58 **Box: World's water in a swimming pool**
The volume of an Olympic swimming pool is 660,000 gallons (https://bit.ly/3etTH3V). Using *National Geographic*'s estimate that only .025% of the world's fresh water is accessible (https://on.natgeo.com/32Qfttv), that leaves us with just 165 gallons—not even enough water to completely fill the 200-gallon capacity of a 3-person hot tub (https://bit.ly/2S6ZYey), let alone for Katie Ledecky to win a gold medal in.

60 **Box: Desert ants' marathon food trek**
The left-hand side of the box is a direct quote from the groundbreaking book by Arne D. Ekstrom, Hugo J. Spiers, Véronique D. Bohbot, R. Shayna Rosenbaum (2018), *Human Spatial Navigation* (Princeton: Princeton University Press), exploring human cognition and how it forms a basis for our navigational abilities (https://bit.ly/3tUVYvu). The translation helps to contextualize how truly magnificent an ant's senses must be compared to our own: the entire DC metro area has an area of roughly 75 km by 75 km, stretching from Manassas, Virginia, to Prince George's County in Maryland. The distance from the NIH to the Pentagon (https://bit.ly/3sS0k5t) is a mere 30 kilometers (18.5 miles), if you take the long way. Desert ants traverse this equivalent distance and back without so much as a paper map—or a smartphone in their pockets.

61 **Box: Slo-mo fireworks; speed of light vs. speed of sound**
While the speed of light is constant, at 186,282 miles per second (https://bit.ly/3dMSiGK), the speed of sound depends on variables like the matter the sound waves are passing through and the ambient temperature. Let's assume that the New Year's celebration is in Southern California, so the weather is clear and the temperature is around 68°F. Sound under these conditions would travel at about 760 miles per hour (https://bit

.ly/3nmmvQc). If the light from the New Year's fireworks took 10 full seconds to reach the viewer, it would have to be 1,862,000 miles away, a distance that would take a sound wave 102 days to traverse if the laws of physics allowed (we have to suspend the laws of physics, except those related to speed, because anything that far away from Earth would be in space, where sound does not travel). The fireworks display used in this example is almost 8 times farther away from the Earth than the moon is—talk about a grand finale! (https://go.nasa.gov/3ns5KTG)

62 **Box: Black family's penny to White family's dollar in savings**
In 2020, Northwestern University researchers Christine Percheski and Christina Davis took data from the Survey of Consumer Finances to show how economically fragile Black households with children are. This is where we get the penny/dollar figure. The first scenario was inspired by the 2019 Federal Reserve report that 2 in 5 adults in the United States wouldn't be able to come up with $400 in case of an emergency (https://bit.ly/3tVlvoz). Blowing up the penny/dollar gap to real-world size illustrates how dire the discrepancy is: a $2,000 bank balance to a single $20 bill in a pants pocket for a hefty hospital bill. It's half a million in a retirement account vs. just $5,000 to live on indefinitely. Out of the 130 million Americans who visit an emergency room each year (https://bit.ly/3viBfSF), how many are among the 2 in 5 without the means to pay? Christine Percheski and Christina Gibson Davis (2020), "A Penny on the Dollar: Racial Inequalities in Wealth among Households with Children." *Socius: Sociological Research for a Dynamic World.* (https://bit.ly/3dOhMmY)

63 **Box: 5 minutes of Do Now adds 3 weeks of class time**
Taking into account the 180 days per school year (https://bit.ly/3dBDnzv), we can easily work out how 5 minutes extra a day accumulates over the weeks and months, eventually adding up to 540 minutes. Broken up into hours, that's an additional 9 entire class periods. Assuming class is 3 days a week, it's like gaining 3 weeks of class. It's a teacher's dream or a lackluster student's nightmare, but either way it's a lot more time spent learning. The Do Now practice is described in Doug Lemov (2014), *Teach Like a Champion*

2.0: 62 Techniques that Put Students on a Path to College (New York: John Wiley & Sons). (https://bit.ly/3eDsTP4)

64 **Giving up Facebook Fridays**
It's the statistic that none of us wants to believe: that we're collectively spending an average of 2 hours, 22 minutes on social media each day (https://bit.ly/3dO08zF). If you gave up social media on Fridays for only 5 months, you could reclaim about 2,860 minutes (47.6 hours) of your life and use it to do some of the reading you've "never had time for." Reading at an average speed of 238 words per minute (https://bit.ly/2QzqnB4), that would add up to around 676,000 words, easily enough to read the longest classics and at least one of the shortest, too (https://bit.ly/32ORniw; https://bit.ly/3xpPiYq; https://bit.ly/3nmjCyF). A few choice suggestions, all well within the time frame we've laid out:

Under 100,000 words	Under 200,000 words	Under 675,000 words
Entire *Chronicles of Narnia*: 45,535 words	*A Passage to India*: 101,383 words	*Don Quixote*: 344,665 words
The Great Gatsby: 47,094 words	*One Hundred Years of Solitude*: 144,523 words	*Anna Karenina*: 349,736 words
Things Fall Apart: 57,550 words	*Invisible Man*: 160,039 words	Entire *Lord of the Rings* series: 576,459 words
Mrs. Dalloway: 63,422 words	*Jane Eyre*: 183,858 words	*War and Peace*: 587,287 words
The Color Purple: 66,556 words		
Beloved: 88,426 words		

72 **Box: mortality exceeding that of the great plague**
See Edward Tyas Cook (1913), The Life of Florence Nightingale, vol. 1, p. 315. (London: Macmillan)

74 **"planned hospital beds for 10% of its force":** Quote from professor Lynn MacDonald (2014), *History of Statistics: Florence Nightingale and Her*

Crimean War Statistics: Lessons for Hospital Safety, Public Administration and Nursing. (https://bit.ly/3aDqfro)

74 **"The Compassionate Statistician":** Eileen Magnello (2010), "Florence Nightingale: The Compassionate Statistician," *Radical Statistics* 102, pp. 17–32. (https://bit.ly/3xx1O8T)

78 **Box: Great Smoky Mountains National Park**
While 12.5 million visitors sounds like a lot, it also doesn't provide any context. According to the National Parks Service, in 2019 the second-place slot went to the Grand Canyon, with almost 6 million visitors. This pattern has repeated each year since at least 2001: Great Smoky Mountains always ranks number 1, with about twice as many visitors as the Grand Canyon. (https://bit.ly/3sXjJ4S)

80 **The Nile is barely longer than the Amazon:** By many measures, even those made by impartial scientists (https://on.natgeo.com/3tR3yaD), the Amazon is not only the largest river on Earth but also the longest. While the Nile is generally regarded as 6,650 km long (https://bit.ly/3aJI0Fc), measurements of the Amazon range from 6,400 km to 6,992 km, depending on where you place its source and its mouth. At human scale, if the Nile was 6 feet tall, the Amazon would be 5 foot 10 in the traditional (shorter) estimate, but almost 6 foot 4 with the more generous count. In other words, it depends on what shoes the rivers are wearing.

80 **The Amazon is the world's largest river by a substantial margin:** If we were to convert their discharge volume to human weight, it's not even close. If the Nile's average discharge of 2,830 cubic meters per second were an average human weight of 180 pounds, the Amazon, with a flow of 209,000 cubic meters per second (https://bit.ly/2R0Ng06), would weigh in at 13,312, on the high side for a large male bush elephant.

81 **Box: California's economy in the world**
According to Wikipedia, the GDP of California is the fifth largest in the world, eclipsed only by America, China, Japan, and Germany (https://bit.ly/3xr6cWQ). That means that, while the United Nations recognizes 195 sovereign nations in the world, California's economy dwarfs 190 of them.

Makes you think twice about laughing when Californians talk about se-
cession, doesn't it? Incidentally, the American economy would still be the
largest in the world, even without California.

82 **Wealth of Apple Nation**
According to Credit Suisse's Global Wealth Report Databook, in 2019
only 21 countries had total wealth of $2 trillion or more (https://bit
.ly/3aDpxue). The United States is the only country whose total wealth
stretches to 15 digits, with $106 trillion in total wealth, while China is
hot behind with $64 trillion, followed by Japan at $25 trillion and Germany at $15 trillion. Some countries, like Mexico and Brazil, make the list
largely by virtue of their large populations, while others, like Sweden and
Belgium, see similar levels of total wealth concentrated in a much smaller
population.

82 **Box: If cows were a country**
The Food and Agriculture Organization of the United Nations claims
that livestock are responsible for 14.5% of all CO_2 emissions (https://
bit.ly/3aEIzAh), and cows are to blame for 62% of that figure (https://bit
.ly/3vqGNuF), which means that our big-eyed buddies are pumping out
around 9% of total global greenhouse-gas emissions each year. So, in global
output terms, starting at the top with mega-emitter China (28%), then the
United States (15%), coming in third is . . . cows. India, at 7%, comes in
fourth. (https://bit.ly/3noaRny). The "cows as a country: phrase is a Steven
Chu quote from: Tad Friend (2019). "Can a Burger Help Solve Climate
Change?" *The New Yorker* September 30, 2019.

84 **Dwight Eisenhower's famous "Chance for Peace" speech:** Delivered
shortly after Stalin's death, and also known as the "Cross of Iron" speech,
it was a historic admonition against war spending. The full text is available
via the Eisenhower library. (https://bit.ly/3gGhwYX)

85 **Box: Fruit juice vs. donuts, a symphony in sugar**
Cranberry juice seems like a healthy bet. That's why it's so shocking to
discover that a 12-oz. serving of Ocean Spray Cran-Apple, the size of a
standard soft drink can clock in with 44 grams of sugar. That's more

For more, see heathbrothers.com/mnc/webnotes.

sugar than you would consume by eating 3 glazed Krispy Kreme donuts at 30 grams of sugar (https://bit.ly/3sQMDDJ) plus 3 sugar cubes (at 4 grams apiece, https://bit.ly/32N0gsS). Clearly, you should save one of those sugar cubes for a coffee with your 3 donuts and skip the juice.

86 **270,000 patients a year die from sepsis:** Based on data from the National Institutes of Health. (https://bit.ly/3sNvHhz)

86 **reduces sepsis deaths by 55%:** Sourced from Kaiser Permanente data analysis, B. Crawford, M. Skeath, and A. Whippy, "Kaiser Permanente Northern California sepsis mortality reduction initiative," *Crit Care* 16, P12 (2012). (https://bit.ly/2QWOedV)

86 **every woman with breast cancer and every man with prostate cancer:** In 2019, 42,281 females died of breast cancer, 31,638 males died of prostate cancer, 45,886 people died of pancreatic cancer, and 27,959 people died of liver cancer: 147,764 in total. Source: CDC website. (https://bit.ly/3vlTA1m)

The version in the chapter tells only half the story, the lifesaving capacity of the sepsis intervention is even stronger than the comparisons so far. In reality the intervention could save "every woman with breast cancer, every man with prostate cancer, and every single patient with pancreatic or liver cancer . . . combined."

Why not include these in the final version in the chapter? It's a judgment call, and we may have made the wrong decision. But we suspect that testing would find that people would be readier to take action in response to the simpler, breast versus prostate cancer comparison. They have a clear playbook for getting the attention of the medical community.

87 **World's most populous cities:** This statistic makes use of the UN's list of the 81 world cities that have more than 5 million in population (https://bit.ly/3gG7E1x). London and Paris are around 10 million each, Barcelona is 5 million. Shanghai, the largest city in China, has as many people as these three European cities combined.

90 **Box: What are the odds of being diagnosed with a mental illness?** The number of adults diagnosed with a mental illness each year is estimated at 1 in 4 by Johns Hopkins (https://bit.ly/2LDDQoB) and at 1 in

5 by the National Institute of Mental Health (https://bit.ly/3opOWfD). However, the likelihood of being diagnosed with a mental illness over the course of a lifetime is 1 in 2, according to the Centers for Disease Control (https://bit.ly/386MPHw). For every 10 people in a room, 2 could be expected to be diagnosed with a mental illness in the coming year, but 5 out of 10 will be diagnosed at some point in their lives.

90 **Box: Kenya vs. America—food expenditure as a proportion of income**
According to CEIC data (https://bit.ly/3uQuQif), Kenyans earned an average of about $7,000 in 2019, while the median American household income in 2019 was $68,700, according to the U.S. Census Bureau (https://bit.ly/3b8VLxY). If Americans, like Kenyans, spent around half their earnings on food (https://bit.ly/3v3Ycsy), they would spend about $660 on food each week. This scenario was inspired by a fact in Mike Fairbrass and David Tanguy's 2017 *The Scale of Things* (Quadrille Publishing).

91 **Box: The billionaire's staircase**
According to the U.S. Census (https://bit.ly/3vgY9do), 50% of Americans (and almost 90% of people, https://bit.ly/3kKgDi6) have a household wealth of less than $100,000 (Credit Suisse Global Wealth Report, https://bit.ly/3hS5A4Y), so 1 in 2 never take the first step up the staircase. Just under 25% of Americans have a net worth over $427,000, so only 1 in 4 get to the fourth step. Fewer than 1 in 10 Americans will reach the tenth step, the $1 million mark. When we divide Bezos's $198,000,000,000 (https://bit.ly/3vgY9do) by $100,000, we're looking at 1,930,000 steps. So if you spend 2 months climbing stairs for 9 hours each day at a rate of 61 steps per minute (a below-average rate, according to researchers, https://bit.ly/2LbIxX2), you could eventually reach his level of wealth. Better get some supportive shoes!

92 **Box: The Prius highlight reel**
The average American drives about 40 miles per day, according to the Department of Transportation (https://bit.ly/3rk0ti7). If your car gets the typical 25 miles per gallon suggested by the EPA (https://bit.ly/3uUE25g), when you replace it with a Prius, you stand to save half of the money you're spending monthly on fuel: at $3 per gallon, you save $72 per month, or $864 per year.

For more, see heathbrothers.com/mnc/webnotes.

96 **Box: Batter meets clapper, an illustration**
Acoustic scientist Bruno Repp found that the average adult can clap around 4 times per second (https://bit.ly/3uYnNUJ). That gives us 250 milliseconds per clap. A 90-mile-per-hour fastball takes 400–450 milliseconds to travel from release to the plate, and a swinging bat takes 150 milliseconds to complete its arc (https://bit.ly/3gezhi8). That means a batter only has 250–300 milliseconds (https://n.pr/3hWFRbC) to decide whether or not to swing: just about the time between claps. Of note: the world record for speed-clapping is 1,103 claps per minute, averaging 18.3 claps per second, or 41 milliseconds per clap. (https://bit.ly/3aDEegw)

97 **Box: Fastest 200-meter dash, measured in claps**
When Usain Bolt won the 200-meter dash in the 2016 Olympics with a time of 19.78 seconds, his competitors were within milliseconds of him. Doing 4 claps per second (.25 seconds per clap), if we begin our clap count as Bolt crosses the finish line, the second-place runner crosses .01 seconds before the next clap. By the third clap, the runners in third to seventh place have all crossed, leaving only the eighth-place finisher, who comes in .10 seconds before the fourth clap, hopelessly behind.

97 **Box: National Endowment for the Arts funding per person**
Every time congressional budgets are created, a debate rages around public funding for the arts. In 2016, the NEA was allocated about $148 million (https://bit.ly/3bmcspO) out of a federal budget of $3.9 trillion (https://bit.ly/3esWj2c). Dividing the NEA allocation by the federal budget, it comes out to about .004% of the total budget. If a typical American earning $60,000 a year pays around $6,300 in federal taxes (https://bit.ly/3v4Yu3e), their contribution is 25 cents, or one shiny quarter.

99 **Box: 3 women, 1 man as legislature**
According to the Pew Research Center (https://pewrsr.ch/3rtD91l), despite the fact that the largest number of women in history were elected to the House of Representatives in 2020, women still only fill 27% of congressional seats. To illustrate this imbalance to a room full of people, create a group of 3 women to 1 man and then instruct the women to vote on policies that would affect men specifically. As Nick

For more, see heathbrothers.com/mnc/webnotes.

Ferroni brilliantly illustrates, the results speak for themselves. (https:// bit.ly/2MYLsDs)

99 **Box: Jeff Bezos's 11-second earnings**
In 2020, the net worth of Jeff Bezos increased by $75 billion (https://bit.ly/3ec01yG), leaving him worth around $188 billion at year's end. Dividing $75 billion by 365 days gives us $205 million per day. Further dividing that by 24 hours leaves us with a mere $8.5 million per hour. Divide that by 60 minutes and it becomes about $143,000 per minute, which further breaks down to around $2,400 per second. In 11 seconds, Jeff Bezos made just over $26,000.

100 **Box: Gloves on the board room table**
This story is told by Jon Stegner in the book by John P. Kotter and Dan S. Cohen (2012), *The Heart of Change: Real-life Stories of how People Change Their Organizations* (Cambridge: Harvard Business Review Press).

102 **Box: VC investment in Silicon Valley**
Writer Russ Mitchell lays out how, in order to make an 18% annual return on the $252 billion in VC funds tied up in tech start-ups, it would take more than 325 eBays to yield $1.3 trillion in investor value by the end of the period in 10 years' time—2.7 per month, for a total of 10 years (https://cnn.it/3aYvXEr). The 2010s version of this would be between 2 and 3 Facebooks undergoing an initial public stock offering per month, for the remainder of the decade. (https://nyti.ms/3 gFypDf)

103 **Paul Slovic has studied how our compassion:** Recalling the methods of Florence Nightingale, Paul Slovic notes in his research that dry statistics fail to move people in the way that individual, relatable stories are able to. His work details how mass tragedies fail to elicit appropriate emotional responses, and how the "emotional blurring" of compassion fatigue starts the moment we shift the focus from 1 life to 2. Paul Slovic and Daniel Västfjäll (2015), "The More Who Die, the Less We Care: Psychic Numbing and Genocide," *Imagining Human Rights*, pp. 55–68 (De Gruyter) (https:// bit.ly/32MciCY); Paul Slovic (2007), "'If I Look at the Mass I Will Never

For more, see heathbrothers.com/mnc/webnotes.

Act': Psychic Numbing and Genocide," *Judgment and Decision Making* 2:2, pp. 79–95. (https://bit.ly/3tVchZd)

103 **Box: Revisiting firearms**
According to the Census Clock, a new baby is born in the United States every 9 seconds (https://bit.ly/3nor4co). Because there are about 31.5 million seconds in the year, we can calculate that about 3.5 million babies will be born in that time. When we take our 70 million surplus firearms (https://wapo.st/3tT6547) and deliver each gift-wrapped to our newborns, it will take us almost 20 years to exhaust our supply.

104 **Familiar measurements:** "The distance covered while drinking a young coconut." Kensy Cooperrider and Dedre Gentner (2019), "The career of measurement," *Cognition* 191. (https://bit.ly/3nmpqbq)

105 **Box: Charles Fishman's water bottle**
Charles Fishman (2007), "Message in a Bottle," *Fast Company*, July/August (https://bit.ly/3sMQoKs). Using contemporary prices for Evian and Yosemite water as delivered by San Francisco, we could refill the bottle for 4.5 years.

105 **Box: Six Sigma**
Wikipedia. (https://bit.ly/3bUCnVD)

105 **Without giving up a single hit:** A typical benchmark for an outstanding starting pitcher is to reach 200 innings in a season (https://bit.ly/3euQIIJ), and most pitchers throw about 15 pitches per inning (https://atmlb.com/32R8DDP), which adds up to about 3,000 pitches per season. That means you would have to go 98 seasons between making a mistake (whether missing the strike zone or giving up a hit).

106 **Box: Murders by minutes vs. murders per day**
According to the CDC, there are 19,141 homicides per year in the United States (https://bit.ly/3r38qr6). Divided by 365 days of the year, that gives us a little over 52 deaths per day. Broken up into 24 hours in a day, that means that 2 people are murdered every hour, or 1 every 30 minutes. 2 per hour feels like the rate of murders being resolved on the typical detective

show on television, but visualizing a daily total of 52 people filling the first few rows of a movie theater—it carries weight.

But wait! What happened to focusing on 1? Good question: In that chapter, we recommended that you try focusing on 1 first, because it is the simplest solution. Here, though, we tried focusing on 1 and it fell short emotionally. When that happens, it is good to have other techniques to fall back on.

110 Box: American diets vs. available land on earth

According to *Our World in Data*, it would take 138% of our habitable land to raise enough cows, pigs, and chickens to feed everyone in the world like Americans feed themselves (https://bit.ly/2Nsr6m9). There are 104 million square km of habitable land in the world and we would have to use all of it to feed everyone an American diet—converting all of our suburban yards and softball fields into cow farms and learning to raise chickens in all of our home basements and office buildings. But even that wouldn't be enough. We also need to add 38% more land. 38% more than the 104 million square km of habitable land is 35.5 million square km. *The World Atlas* lists total area of Africa at 30 million square km and Australia at 8.5 million square km (https://bit.ly/3eT95Jd). Adding them together provides slightly more than the 35.5 million square km we'd need to feed the world an American diet. (But even this underestimates the additional area needed because it assumes that every square kilometer of Australia and Africa is habitable.)

110 Box: Odds of Winning Powerball

To really put massively unlikely odds into context, take the 1-in-292,201,338 odds of winning the Powerball jackpot (https://bit.ly/2RUdAJR) and divide 292,201,338 by 300, resulting in 974,000. Breaking that into days gives us 2,666 years, a hard but not impossible number to grasp. What makes the encore effective in this example is that if we merely imagined someone having to guess one out of 292,201,338 possible days, the range would extend for 800,020 years and 33 days. That would mean that the unlucky guesser would have to select a date from between January 1 in the year 1 and February 2 in the year 800,020. While the year 2,666 feels somewhat far-fetched, it's at least in the same millennium we're living in—widen the scope another couple of hundred thousand years and the number gets too big to really appreciate how unlikely winning the jackpot would be.

111 **Box: Air Frogger**
The distance a frog can jump varies a great deal by species, but according to the Field Museum in Chicago, the northern leopard frog can jump 15 times its body length (https://bit.ly/3aDjeXA). Since an average American is 5 foot 6 (https://bit.ly/2Qy4t1h), leaping like a bullfrog would make possible a jumping distance of 82 feet, way more than you'd need to cover the 66 feet between one 3-point line on an NBA court and the opposite side's basket (https://on.nba.com/2PmvaFD). Not only is that farther than any professional basketball player could ever hope to cover in a single jump, it's about twice as far as Steph Curry's world-beating shooting range—though once in a career he might sink a shot that long, as a last-second heave. (https://bit.ly/2QXDYlw)

113 **Box: Steve Jobs introduces the MacBook Air**
The best source for this is an edited 4-minute video that can be found at (https://bit.ly/3gk8Bux). The reversal slide, however, is only found on the longer, hour-plus version of his presentation.

114 **Romeo Santos sells out Yankee Stadium times 2:** Larry Rohter, July 10, 2014, *New York Times*, July 10, 2014.

116 **How do people in the world feel about free trade:** Sourced from Fareed Zakaria, "New consensus on value of trade, US is the odd man out." *Newsweek*, October 22, 2007 (https://bit.ly/3tT7yat). Zakaria was reporting on a study by the Pew Institute, *World Publics Welcome Global Trade—But Not Immigration*, 47-Nation Pew Global Attitudes Survey October 4, 2007. (https://pewrsr.ch/3eyGGpL)

117 **Box: Globe-spanning giant**
The quotation describing neuroscientist David Linden's analogy is taken from p. 198 of Joel Levy's 2018 *The Big Book of Science: Facts, Figures, and Theories to Blow Your Mind* (New York: Chartwell Books) (https://bit.ly/2QY1vTx). This book is filled with interesting number translations. Joel Levy has a great eye and uses engaging graphics. Buy this book if you

For more, see heathbrothers.com/mnc/webnotes.

want to provide your junior-high or high-school students with the wonder of a *Guinness Book of World Records* and also want them to learn something important about the world.

122 **"No one that cold had ever lived."**
Case study taken from Michael Blastland and David Spiegelhalter (2014), *The Norm Chronicles: Stories and Numbers About Danger and Death*. (New York: Basic Books) p 15. (https://bit.ly/32RjnlC)

122 **At 50, we won't let you travel:** This is from a case study of Brian Zikmund-Fisher's decision whether to undergo a bone marrow transplant when he was a 28-year-old graduate student. He survived the operation and is now a professor at the University of Michigan Medical School, teaching, among other things, risk communication. Chip Heath and Dan Heath (2013), *Decisive: How to Make Better Choices in Life and Work* (New York: Crown Business) pp. 120–26.

123 **Box: Condensed history of the universe**
When Carl Sagan condensed the history of the universe into a single year for his landmark documentary series *Cosmos*, the big bang of his Cosmic Calendar occurred on January 1 (https://bit.ly/3tXlBfu). It wasn't until May that the Milky Way was formed, and the sun and earth didn't come into being until the middle of September. Life evolved across the next few months until the very end of December, when the first humans arrived. No matter what time scale you use, the takeaway is clear: humans themselves are a very, very recent addition to the cosmos, and our recorded history—which only stretches back some 5,000 years—an even smaller fraction of everything that has ever happened.

126 **Box: Tax year**
This calculation was way harder than it should have been, because there is no single source that looks at what a voter pays in taxes and gives a whole picture of where and how much is devoted to various programs. How are we supposed to have a national conversation about an appropriate budget if it took five experienced researchers to cobble together the data on this page a little at a time? We also had the assistance of the wonderful Lee Roberts, who is budget director for the State of North Carolina and teaches the graduate public budgeting class at Duke's public policy school.

For more, see heathbrothers.com/mnc/webnotes.

The best summary we have found is this one from the Congressional Budget Office: (https://bit.ly/3ey3Ooj).

In 2018, total budget expenditures equaled $4.1 trillion:

$982 billion for Social Security (24%)

$971 billion for Medicare [$582] + Medicaid[$389] (24%)

$325 billion in interest payments on the national debt (8%)

Combined, over half of the nation's annual budget is devoted to the three categories above, which are sometimes called "nondiscretionary," although what that means is that they are not changeable in the short run but are changeable in the medium to long run. There are also two categories of "discretionary" spending:

$623 billion on national defense (16%)

$639 billion on non-defense discretionary spending (16%)

The last category is the most interesting. "Non-defense discretionary" spending is only 16% of the budget but it encapsulates almost all of the functions we normally think of as "government" at the national level: NASA space flights, FDA meat inspections, FBI investigations, FAA air traffic controllers. Here are some other specific expenses that fall in this category:

$149 billion invested in higher ed (3.6%)

$68 billion on SNAP (food stamps) and other food assistance (1.7%)

$3.26 billion on national parks (.08%)

$19 billion for NASA (.46%)

[The numbers reviewed above don't add to $4.1 trillion because there are a few types of "other" expenses, including retirement plans for the military and government employees and some veterans' benefits.]

129 **Box: Workplace productivity**
Symbolic soccer game taken from the pages of Stephen Covey (2004), *The 8th Habit: From Effectiveness to Greatness* (New York: Simon & Schuster).

133 ***How to Lie with Statistics:*** The title was tongue-in-cheek, but ironically Huff later got paid professionally to lie with statistics on behalf of the tobacco industry, as detailed in Alex Reinhart's 2014 article "Huff and Puff." (https://bit.ly/3aFrYMJ)

For more, see heathbrothers.com/mnc/webnotes.

INDEX

ABOUT THE AUTHORS

Chip Heath is a professor at Stanford Graduate School of Business. Chip and his brother, Dan, have written four *New York Times* bestselling books: *Made to Stick*, *Switch*, *Decisive*, and *The Power of Moments*. He has helped more than 530 start-ups refine and articulate their strategies and mission. Chip lives in Los Gatos, California.

Karla Starr has written for *O, The Oprah Magazine*; *The Atlantic*; *Slate*; and *Popular Science*, and has appeared on *CBS Sunday Morning*. She lives in Portland, Oregon.